Becoming a Travel Professional: The Complete Guide

Becoming a Travel Professional: The Complete Guide

Joseph Sawyer

STATES
ACADEMIC PRESS
www.statesacademicpress.com

Becoming a Travel Professional: The Complete Guide
Joseph Sawyer
ISBN: 978-1-63989-071-2 (Hardback)

STATES
ACADEMIC PRESS

Published by States Academic Press,
109 South 5th Street,
Brooklyn, NY 11249, USA

Cataloging-in-Publication Data

Becoming a travel professional : the complete guide / Joseph Sawyer.
p. cm.
Includes bibliographical references and index.
ISBN 978-1-63989-071-2
1. Travel agents--Guidebooks. 2. Business travel consultants--Guidebooks.
3. Tourism--Guidebooks. I. Sawyer, Joseph.
G154 .B43 2021
338.479 1--dc23

For more information regarding States Academic Press and its products, please visit the publisher's website www.statesacademicpress.com

Table of Contents

Preface

Travel professionals manage and handle a client's travel needs. A travel professional is an expert of travel and hospitality. They provide specialized services that aid in the reservation of tickets, hotels and other travel particulars. They also provide details about local attractions, events and specialties. Managing cars, flights, trains, hotels, etc. is an important function of a travel professional. Meeting a client's expectations and interests within budget and time schedule is a vital aspect of the travel and hospitality industry. This book explores all the important aspects of professional travel and tourism in the present day scenario. Coherent flow of topics, student-friendly language and extensive use of examples make this book an invaluable source of knowledge.

Given below is the chapter wise description of the book:

Chapter 1- A travel agency provides services related to tourism and travel. They coordinate with airlines, cars, hotels, resorts, etc. to manage an individual's travel needs. They also provide travel package tours that focus on particular aspects of travel. This chapter has been carefully written to provide an easy understanding of the varied facets of the travel industry.

Chapter 2- Traveling on a budget requires careful planning and consideration must be given about food and drink, lodging and duration. Budget travel has limitations but it is an upcoming trend to visit another region or go on a holiday without spending a lot of money. Budget travel is best understood in confluence with the major topics listed in the following chapter.

Chapter 3- Travel agents book tickets that would enable customers to travel to the venue or region of their choice. Sticking to a budget should be an important concern for the travel agent. Emergencies such as cancellation of flights, changes in schedule, etc. are situations that a travel agent must be prepared for. The aspects elucidated in this chapter are of vital importance, and provide a better understanding of ticket booking.

Chapter 4- The travel agent must keep in mind the choices and tastes of the customer along with the ambience and services provided by the hotel while making reservations. The customer's budget is an important factor while booking hotels. Hotel reservation management is best understood in confluence with the major topics listed in the following chapter.

At the end, I would like to thank all those who dedicated their time and efforts for the successful completion of this book. I also wish to convey my gratitude towards my friends and family who supported me at every step.

Joseph Sawyer

CHAPTER 1 Understanding Principles of Travel Industry

A travel agency provides services related to tourism and travel. They coordinate with airlines, cars, hotels, resorts, etc. to manage an individual's travel needs. They also provide travel package tours that focus on particular aspects of travel. This chapter has been carefully written to provide an easy understanding of the varied facets of the travel industry.

Travel Agency

A travel agency is a private retailer or public service that provides travel and tourism related services to the public on behalf of suppliers such as activities, airlines, car rentals, cruise lines, hotels, railways, travel insurance, and package tours. In addition to dealing with ordinary tourists most travel agencies have a separate department devoted to making travel arrangements for business travelers and some travel agencies specialize in commercial and business travel only. There are also travel agencies that serve as general sales agents for foreign travel companies, allowing them to have offices in countries other than where their headquarters are located.

Operations

A travel agency's main function is to act as an agent, selling travel products and services on behalf of a supplier. Consequently, unlike other retail businesses, they do not keep a stock in hand, unless they have pre-booked hotel rooms and/or cabins on a cruise ship for a group travel event such as a wedding, honeymoon, or a group event. A package holiday or a ticket is not purchased from a supplier unless a customer requests that purchase. The holiday or ticket is supplied to the agency at a discount. The profit is therefore the difference between the advertised price which the customer pays and the discounted price at which it is supplied to the agent. This is known as the commission. In many countries, all individuals or companies that sell tickets are required to be licensed as a travel agent.

In some countries, airlines have stopped giving commissions to travel agencies. Therefore, travel agencies are now forced to charge a percentage premium or a standard flat fee, per sale. However, some companies pay travel agencies a set percentage for selling their product. Major tour companies can afford to do this, because if they were to sell a thousand trips at a cheaper rate, they would still come out better than if they sold a hundred trips at a higher rate. This process benefits both parties. It is also cheaper to offer commissions to travel agents rather than engage in advertising and distribution campaigns without using agents.

Other commercial operations are undertaken, especially by the larger chains. These can include the sale of in-house insurance, travel guide books, and public transport timetables, car rentals, and the services of an on-site bureau de change, dealing in the most popular holiday currencies.

Travel agents in Rio de Janeiro, Brazil

A travel agent is supposed to offer impartial travel advice to the customer, as well as coordinating travel details and assisting the customer in booking travel. However, this function almost disappeared with the mass market package holiday, and some agency chains seemed to develop a "holiday supermarket" concept, in which customers choose their holiday from brochures on racks and then book it from a counter. Again, a variety of social and economic changes have now contrived to bring this aspect to the fore once more, particularly with the advent of multiple, no-frills, low-cost airlines.

Agency Income

Traditionally, travel agencies' principal source of income was, and continues to be, commissions paid for bookings of car rentals, cruise lines, hotels, railways, sightseeing tours, tour operators, etc. A fixed percentage of the main element of the price is paid to the agent as a commission. Commissions may vary depending on the type of product and the supplier. Commissions are not paid on the tax component of the price. Travel agencies also receive a large variety of bonuses, benefits, and other incentives from travel and tourism related companies as inducements for travel agents to promote their products. The customer is normally not made aware of how much the travel agent is earning in commissions and other benefits. Other sources of income may include the sale of insurance, travel guide books, public transport timetables and money exchange.

Since 1995, many airlines around the world and most airlines in the United States now do not pay any commission to travel agencies. In this case, an agency adds a service fee to the net price. Reduced commissions started in 1995 in the United States, with the introduction of a cap of $50 on return trips and $25 on one way. In 1999, European airlines began eliminating or reducing commissions, while Singapore Airlines did so in parts of Asia. In 2002, Delta Air Lines announced a zero-commission base for the U.S. and Canada; after a few months United Airlines, American Airlines, Continental Airlines, Northwest Airlines, US Airways and American Trans Air all followed suit.

Insurance

The majority of travel agents have felt the need to protect themselves and their clients against the possibilities of commercial failure, either their own or a supplier's. They will advertise the fact that they are surety bonded, meaning in the case of a failure, the customers are guaranteed either an equivalent holiday to that which they have lost or, if they prefer, a refund. Many British and American agencies and tour operators are bonded with the International Air Transport Association (IATA), for those who issue air tickets, Air Travel Organisers' Licensing (ATOL) for those who order tickets in, and the Association of British Travel Agents (ABTA) or the American Society of Travel Agents (ASTA), for those who sell package holidays on behalf of a tour company.

Types of Agencies

Allamanda Voyages travel agents in Paris

There are three different types of agencies in the UK: multiples, miniples, and independent agencies. Multiples comprises a number of national chains, often owned by international conglomerates, like Thomson Holidays, now a subsidiary of TUI Group, the German multinational. It is now common for the large mass market tour companies to purchase a controlling interest in a chain of travel agencies, in order to control the distribution of their product. (This is an example of vertical integration.) The smaller chains are often based in particular regions or districts.

Five different types of agencies exist in the United States: independent, host, franchise, consortium, and mega agencies. American Express and the American Automobile Association (AAA) are examples of mega travel agencies. Carlson Wagonlit Travel is an example of a consortium agency consisting of various types of specialty agencies. Expedia CruiseShipCenters is an example of a franchise travel agency, consisting of independently operated travel agencies ran by franchisees. Oasis Agent is an example of a host agency. An example of an independent travel agency, is one that is started by a sole proprietorship, or partnership between individuals that have no business partnerships with competition agencies. Each type of travel agency has its pros and cons.

Independent agencies usually cater to a special or niche market, such as the needs of residents in an upmarket commuter town or suburb, or a particular group interested in a similar activity, such as sporting events, like football, golf, or tennis.

Travel agencies choose between two approaches. One is the traditional, multi-destination, *outbound* travel agency, based in the traveler's originating location; the other is the destination focused, *inbound* travel agency, that is based in the destination and delivers an expertise on that location. At present, the former is usually a larger operator while the latter is often a smaller, independent operator.

Consolidators

Airline consolidators, tour operators, and other types of travel consolidators and wholesalers are high volume sales companies that specialize in selling to niche markets. They may or may not offer various types of services, at a single point of access. These can be hotel reservations, flights or car-rentals. Sometimes the services are combined into vacation packages, that include transfers to the location and lodging. These companies do not usually sell directly to the public, but act as wholesalers to retail travel agencies. Commonly, the sole purpose of consolidators is to sell to ethnic niches in the travel industry. Usually no consolidator offers everything; they may only have contracted rates to specific destinations. Today, there are no domestic consolidators, with some exceptions for business class contracts.

How to Develop a Tourism Business

Tourists are people who travel outside of their home-base environments in order to spend time visiting a different environment in either a business or leisure capacity. Both vacationers and those on business trips are considered tourists, and they may be touring either domestically (within their home country) or internationally. A tourism business is any business that centers on catering to tourists' needs. Follow these steps for how to develop a tourism business.

Steps

1. Decide which sector of tourism you would like to focus your business on. You have several options to choose from when it comes to developing a business in tourism:

- Transportation services. This sector involves transporting tourists to, from and around the tourist destination.
- Travel agencies. Travel agencies are the 1 stop shop for everything involved with visiting a place, including transportation, accommodations and attractions.

- Accommodations. These include hotels, motels, bed and breakfasts, hostels, rental houses, condos and any other place tourists may stay while travelling.
- Guided tours and tour guides. A guided tour service or professional tour guide is a tourism business that specializes in providing informative and entertaining tours through an area's local attractions.
- Hospitality. A hospitality business pertains to any food or beverage establishment that tourists may frequent.

2. Take your geographical location into account. Your local tourist attractions are good indicators of what would and would not make a successful tourism business venture. For example, if your area is secluded from the populace and dense with wineries, then guided winery tours, local bed and breakfasts, and airport transportation services are all viable business options.

3. Size up the competition. Thoroughly research the tourism businesses in your area before you decide which business in tourism is right for you. You will want to choose a tourism sector that is not overly congested, and one that you can contribute something unique to.

4. Write a business plan. Your business plan is the blueprint for your tourism business, and should include the following sections:

- Executive summary. Describe your business's purpose, name, location, personnel needs, tourism business management staff, market sector, competition, marketing plan and financial projections.
- Tourism business summary. This should detail how the business's ownership will be distributed and the start up requirements (funding, assets and location).
- Products and/or services. You need to outline the products and/or services your business will be providing for tourists.
- Analysis of the market. Provide information about your target market and your competition.
- Tourism business strategy. Describe how you plan on running your business, marketing your business and pricing your product or service.
- Financial summary. State your projections for your business's expenses and income.

5. Procure the necessary funds. Present your business plan to potential lenders and/or business partners in order to obtain the start up and operating capital you will need to run your business in tourism.

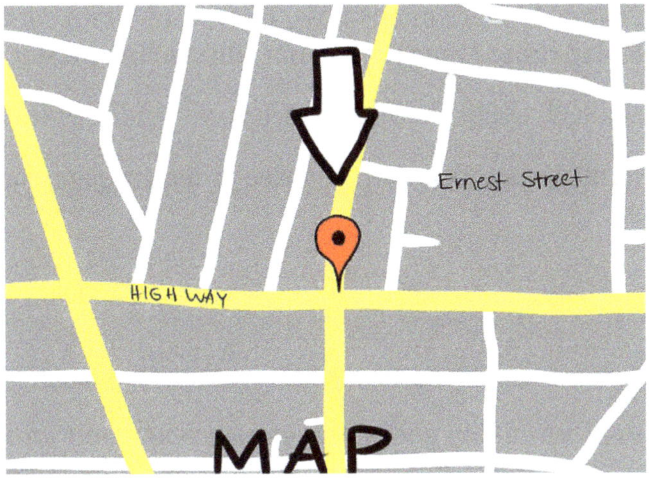

6. Select a business location.

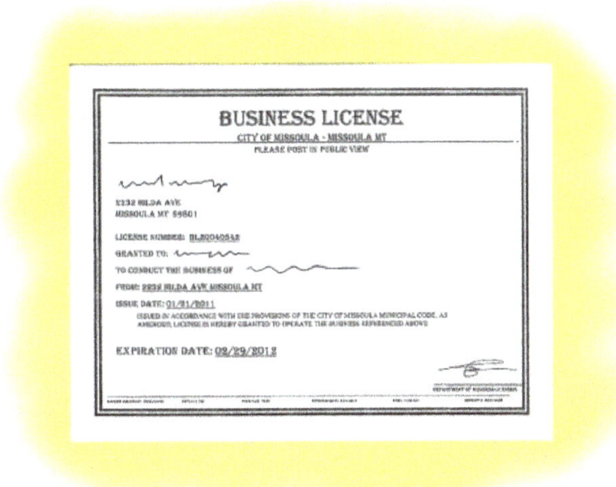

7. Obtain all applicable business licenses. Get the necessary business licensing through your local government's business regulatory agency!

8. Market your tourism business.

- Use social networking sites. Set up accounts/pages on free social networking sites.

- Create a website for your tourism business. Be sure to hire a specialist for search engine optimization (SEO) in order to maximize your site's online presence.
- List your business on all applicable online directories and review websites.
- Advertise in print mediums. Take out ad space in newspapers, magazines and trade/lifestyle publications.

How to Start your Own Business in the Travel Industry

In the modern marketplace, setting up and running a successful and profitable travel business is a highly challenging task. There are a number of ways to enter the travel industry. If you have a love of travel and are planning to have a career in this industry, investing in your own business is a good option.

Method 1

Starting a Franchise Travel Agency

1. Understand the travel industry. First you need to familiarize yourself with different aspects of travel industry. Get as much information as possible about air travel, rail travel, cruises, hotels and vacation destinations. Also learn about what type of travel packages are popular among customers and so on.

- You can search the internet or find books at the local library to help you research the many facets of the travel industry. Additionally, you can directly contact companies in the travel industry, such as cruise ship companies or hotels.
- You may want to consider a niche market depending on your specific location or interests. A niche market is a focus on a specific product or sector of an industry.
- Some niche markets to consider are: cruises, local tours, a specific destination, corporate travel, or travel packages of interest to specific groups of people.

2. Analyze your requirements. A travel franchise business has many benefits. However, each franchiser will have specific requirements, and remember that you will have to split your profits with the franchiser. Each franchiser will provide potential franchisees with their specific requirements.

- There are many different travel agency franchises. Make sure you compare them and their requirements to find the right fit for you and your business. There are many websites and books available to help you learn more about and compare the different franchises available.
- Franchises typically require an initial monetary investment to purchase a franchise. This can be as much as tens of thousands of dollars.

3. Get a franchise license. Obtain travel franchise business licenses and permits of the reputed travel company you chose. The franchise company you choose will provide you with these legal documents. Sign the franchise agreement after proper analysis. Review all the points mentioned in the agreement and ask the franchiser any questions you may have.

- Consider hiring an attorney to review any legal documents included in this process.
- Check with local government agencies for any additional licenses or permits that may be needed.

4. Look for a suitable location. Analyze the location requirements provided by the franchiser and start looking for a location as per those requirements. You will need a good location where clients can come and meet with you. You office must have ample space to house your computers and other essential equipment.

- A real estate agent or website can help you find the right location. If available in your area, try to find a real estate agent who specializes in commercial property.
- The location you choose should be highly visible and traveled by those customers you wish to target.

5. Hire consultants and employees. Like all business ventures, for a travel franchise business you will need to hire an accountant or business consultant to draw up a business plan if you need a loan to get your business started. An accountant will help you to manage your finances effectively. Additional employees may be needed depending on the size or your franchise and the business plan.

- You can find and research professionals, such as accountants, on the internet, in a local phone directory, or through local organizations, such as a chamber of commerce.
- Local staffing agencies or advertisements in local papers can help you find the right employees to make your business a success.

6. Develop marketing strategies: In a franchise travel business, the franchiser will definitely carry out the major advertising and marketing work. However, you will need to do some marketing within your territory to make people aware of your newly established business.

- Consider joining local organizations for business owners, such as a chamber of commerce.
- Compare mass marketing alternatives, including print, radio, and television advertisements, for your target market.
- Include internet and social media marketing in your marketing strategies.
- Build strong relationships with organizations in your industry, such as airlines, cruise ship companies, hotels, and car rental companies. Joint marketing opportunities may be possible.

7. Find Proper payment methods: As in any business, your customers will need to make payments through cash, cheques or credit cards, and you need to make the required arrangements.

- You should open business banking accounts and acquire a credit card that can be used to pay all business related expenses.
- Compare local banking institutions and take advantage of any small business incentives available.

8. Follow franchisor guidelines. Always follow the requirements and guidelines of the franchisor to more effectively achieve your goals. Handle customers efficiently and give importance to the unique selling proposition (USP) of the company.

- The franchisor will provide all of the guidelines and other operating requirements that you need to follow.
- Remember that the franchisor's success depends on the success of its franchisees. Therefore, they are there to help you succeed.

Method 2

Starting a Home-based Travel Agency

1. Check your state and local guidelines to start a home travel agency. Depending on where you live, you may have to file paperwork to legally work from home. You'll also need to file the appropriate paperwork with your local government to become a business.

- You can visit your local government offices to find out more information about these requirements.
- Online research and your local library are other locations to find more information about legal requirements for a small business.

2. Choose the type of home travel agency you want to run. You can do business by referring others to bigger companies, earning a referral fee, or you can do business by booking and selling various travel packages.

- You can search the internet or find books at the local library to help you research the many facets of the travel industry. Additionally, you can directly contact companies in the travel industry, such as cruise ship companies or hotels.
- Contacting other small travel agencies may help you to learn more about the type of agency you want to start.

3. Write a business plan. This will provide you with a solid foundation, and will help you secure funding from investors if you need additional capital to start your business.

- You can find help developing business plans online.
- A business consultant can also help you to develop a solid business plan.

4. Set up banking. You will want to open two separate accounts. One account should be for your

business as an independent travel agent, where you track funds coming in to and going out of the business. The other account should hold all the money your clients provide to book their trips.

- Compare local banking institutions and take advantage of any small business incentives available.
- Aquire a credit or debit card to help pay for business expenses as well.

5. Contact various travel companies. Building relationships with vendors can help you negotiate package deals to offer to your customers.

- Dealing with more than one company can give you more to offer your clients, and it could also provide you with additional money.
- Having strong relationships in the industry can also help your marketing efforts.

6. Market your business. As opposed to franchisees or independent contractors, home-based travel agencies need to perform all of their own marketing.

- Consider joining local organizations for business owners, such as a chamber of commerce.
- Compare mass marketing alternatives, including print, radio, and television advertisements, for your target market.
- Include internet and social media marketing in your marketing strategies.
- Consider partnering with other travel agencies that can serve as your connection between

the airlines, cruise lines, and accommodations. With these connections, you can have additional time to make more connections in the industry.

Method 3

Becoming and Independent Contractor in the Travel Industry

1. Research different host agencies. Independent contractors in the travel industry may have the best of both worlds. They have the independence of their own business with the backing and security of a host agency, which pays a commission to the contractor.

- There are many different host agencies. Make sure you compare them and their requirements to find the right fit for you and your business.
- You can search the internet or find books at the local library to help you research different host agencies in the travel industry.
- Some host agencies require an initial monetary investment to become an independent contractor. However, the cost is typically much less than purchasing a franchise.
- Host agencies handle much of the back office work, such as calculating and paying commissions, providing training, and handling some marketing.
- Licensing and certification are typically handled by the hosting agency, allowing the independent contractor to focus on finding customers and making sales.

2. Sign a contract agreement with the selected host agency. The host agency will provide you with

the legal documents. Review the agreement thoroughly before signing. Ask the host agency any questions you may have.

- Consider hiring an attorney to review any legal documents included in this process.
- Check with local government agencies for any additional licenses or permits that may be needed.

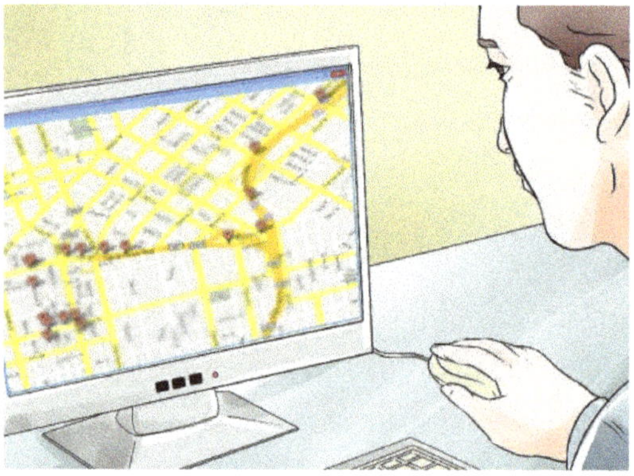

3. Consider your business location. Independent contractors are not employees of the host agency. They are their own business owners. Some host agencies do provide office space for their contractors. You may also consider a home-based office or a traditional store front office.

- A real estate agent or website can help you find the right location. If available in your area, try to find a real estate agent who specializes in commercial property.
- The location you choose should be highly visible and traveled by those customers you wish to target.

4. Follow host agency guidelines. Be sure to understand and follow any requirements from your host agency. As much as possible, take advantage of any training offered by the host agency, as this will help you meet their expectations and achieve your own goals.

- The host agency will provide all of the guidelines and other operating requirements that you need to follow.
- Remember that the host agency's success depends on the success of its independent contractors. Therefore, they are there to help you succeed.

How to Start a Travel Agency from Home

If you are an experienced traveler with a background in sales and/or travel booking and you are looking for opportunities to work from home, consider starting your own home-based travel agency. The travel industry is a strong economic sector, but travel booking is also a service many people would rather perform themselves. Running your own travel agency from home comes with a unique set of challenges and perks, so before jumping in, make sure it's the right move for you.

Part 1

Getting Started

1. Check local and state laws. Before you start working as a home-based travel agent, you need to make sure you comply with all applicable laws concerning home-based business and travel booking. Depending on where you live, you may have to file paperwork to legally work from home. You will also likely need to file appropriate paperwork to become established as a recognized business in your state.

- Look for your state's business zoning laws online.

2. Develop a business plan. Not only will this provide you with a clear plan for running your agency, but it will help you secure funding from investors if you need additional capital to start your business. If you want to get financial backing for your agency, your business plan will need to in-

clude a great deal of information about your plans and projected financial information. For tips on how to create a business plan, check out How to Write a Business Plan.

- Don't forget to state your personal licenses, degrees, skills, and qualifications in your business plan. This information should include essentially anything you would put in a resume. For purposes of obtaining financing (if needed), you will need to show your potential lender that you are capable of assuming responsibility for your business.

3. Identify a target audience. Do some online research to figure out what demographic is likely to be most interested in your services and plan to target them specifically. You should use your target audience to help you figure out how to market your business. For instance, if you are targeting retirees, you should probably not rely solely on social media for advertising.

- Analyze demographic information for your area, which can be found at your city or county auditor's office or website.
- Find travel statistics for your proposed specialty area and also find out what proportion of people near you fit your target demographic.
- Use these data to estimate your anticipated business over a given period and what your profit might be.

4. Anticipate start-up needs. Create a detailed list of what you require (equipment, supplies, employees, etc.) in order to begin business operations. For each item in your list, include a justification for its need and its estimated cost. This information should also go into your business plan.

- Since your business will be run from your home, you may find that you already have many of the items or materials you will need to operate your travel agency (such as basic office supplies). However, you might wish to keep your personal and business materials separate for tax reasons.
- Keep receipts for everything you purchase for your business so you can include them as tax write-offs.

5. Calculate projected cash flow. Consider all your likely financial obligations; this might include insurance premiums, business licensure, and applicable taxes. Then consider your projected income, which should be based on current travel market data and on the presence of your local target demographic. This sort of information will be a critical component of your business plan, but will also help you figure out whether your home travel agency will be viable.

- Be sure to do your homework on this so you don't overestimate your likely earnings.
- Don't forget to account for one-time and/or emergency expenses. For example, perhaps some of your expenses during the first few months of operation will not recur.

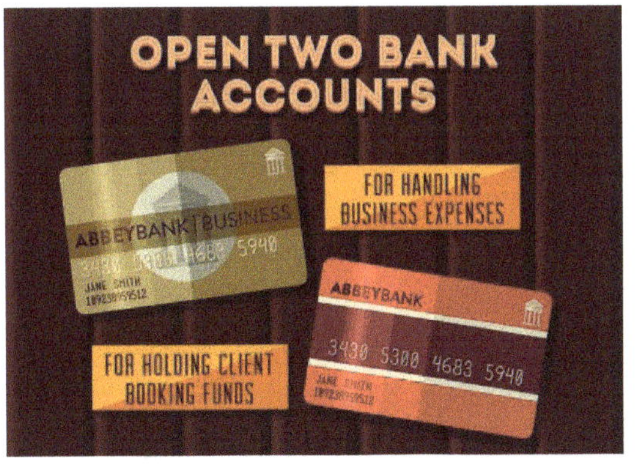

6. Open two bank accounts. One account is for your business and will serve the purpose of handling business expenses and receiving all income. The other account is for holding all your client booking funds, which will be allocated specifically to covering the expenses associated with your clients' travel arrangements.

- It is a good idea to select a financial institution that has special deals for small businesses (such as rewards or waived annual account fees).

- For ease of tracking and transferring funds when necessary, have both bank accounts be through the same banking institution.
- For tax and legal reasons, do not combine your business accounts with your personal checking or savings accounts.

7. Choose a travel specialty. Consider whether you'd rather operate a general travel booking agency or have a more specialized business niche. You can do business by referring others to bigger companies (thereby earning a referral fee), or you can focus on booking and selling specialized travel packages. There are tons of options here.

- As a home travel agent, you could focus solely on cruises, vacation homes, luxury travel, or standard travel specializing in booking flights and hotels.
- Consider whether you wish to specialize in a certain geographical area. You might be able to offer unique services or deals not found elsewhere by doing repeat business with a handful of resorts (for example).
- Draw from your personal expertise and/or experience in choosing a specialty. Going with what you know is often a solid decision.

Part 2

Creating a Home Office Space

1. Check regulations in your area. In order to have customers visit your home for business purpos-

es, you may have to comply with certain health, fire, and building codes pertaining to your home office. It is even possible that you will not be able to establish a home office without a separate entrance for your office and a minimum square footage for your space. Check your city and state government websites for specific information.

- You may also have to comply with Americans with Disabilities Act (ADA) regulations for your home office, which could include making your home office accessible to wheelchairs.
- Certain safety precautions may be required for your office space, such as having a smoke detector and/or a fire extinguisher in the room.

2. Designate a room for work only. Your home office should be a dedicated area within your home that is used solely for business purposes. This conveys professionalism to your customers, who probably don't want to see your kids' toys strewn across the floor of your office. If possible, select a room in your home close to the building entrance so your customers don't have to trek through your house to get there.

- Whether or not your local or state building codes require it, having a separate entrance for your office space is a great feature, as it helps keep your home and work spaces separate and preserves your family's privacy.
- Put a lock on the door that lead from your home into your office. This will keep children, house guests, etc. from getting into your workspace when they shouldn't.

3. Purchase a desk. You will need to have a desk in your home office that you can sit behind while

working with customers. In addition to appearing professional, this is a functional necessity as your transactions will involve document signing and possibly pamphlet or brochure material viewing.

- Make sure your desk is large enough to be useful, yet small enough to fit comfortably in your office. Cramming an enormous desk into a tiny room will make the area feel too small and could create awkward experience for your customers.
- Get a flat-top executive-style desk with no built-in pieces on top that would be positioned between you and your customers. You want your office space to seem as uncluttered as possible.
- While a desk is an important office accessory, you should also leave room for additional essentials, such as a filing cabinet and chairs for your customers.

4. Decorate tastefully. While a minimal amount of artwork and knick-knacks are acceptable, try not to overdo it when decorating your home office. As a travel agent, it might be a good idea to decorate with photos or paintings of picturesque landscapes of places to which you offer travel arrangements.

- Reserve some wall space for any diplomas or certificates you have received (especially those relevant to your work as a travel agent). Frame these and hang them on the wall behind your desk or next to where your customers will be seated.
- Add some plants to your office to make your office feel more comfortable and inviting. Plants add color and help freshen the air; just be sure they don't get so big they encroach on your workspace.

5. Keep it clean and organized. Perhaps the most important thing you can do for your home of-

fice to maintain an image of professionalism is to ensure that it is well-organized and clean. This means tidying up regularly, dusting and vacuuming at least every few days, and emptying trash bins at the end of each work day.

- Make your office a cleaning priority; most of us occasionally allow our homes to fall into disarray when we are busy or overworked, but customers expect to see cleanliness and order in a professional office, even if it is in someone's home.
- A customer who finds your workspace to be cluttered and disorganized may be hesitant to entrust you with their travel arrangements; professionalism is the name of the game here!

Part 3

Maximizing your Business and Profit

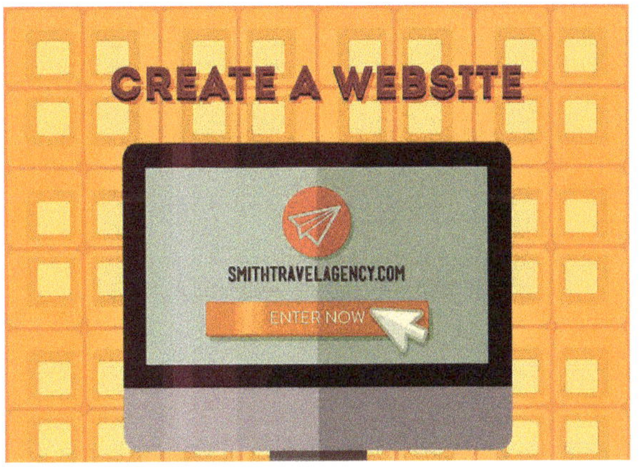

1. Create a website. This is essential for the successful operation of an at-home travel agency, because the majority of your business (including most of your initial contact with clients) will be conducted online. Additionally, having a well-maintained website conveys professionalism to potential clients and is the best way to have your business discovered by interested customers.

- You can create a website for free using a number of services, including OnlineAgency.com.

2. Look into referrals. Contact large, well-established travel companies to negotiate package deals that you can offer to your clients. Some large companies will allow you to operate privately as a

contractor, but only if you comply with their regulations and licensure. While you're at it, ask what kind of referral commissions you can earn by sending customers their way.

- If you choose to operate under a "host agency," you may have to check with them regarding your freedom to have a referral relationship with other companies.
- Referrals are a good option to keep open because it can both offer your clients a wider range of travel options and give you more chances to increase your profits.
- Contact multiple companies and try to establish relationships with all of them. The more companies you work with, the more business you will likely see.

3. Join professional travel agent organizations. These organizations can increase your visibility to consumers and your credibility as an agent. You can join the American Society of Travel Agents (ASTA), the National Association of Commissioned Travel Agents (NACTA), or the International Air Transport Association (IATA). If possible, join all 3 to give your business the biggest boost.

- Professional organizations such as these allow you access to educational materials such as webinars and online discussion forums and hold annual conferences you can attend to learn about new developments in the travel industry.
- Some organization websites have cycling membership features, which (should you be featured) would be massively helpful for increasing your visibility as an agent.
- Some particularly shrewd customers might look for agents who belong to these memberships so they know they are dealing with a vetted professional.
- Check to make sure that your name and business contact information can be found online in organization databases. If your name can't be found on the organization website, then being a member won't increase your visibility much.
- Most professional organizations require an annual membership fee, so build this into your financial projections/business plan if you intend to join any.
- Determine whether you need to meet additional requirements for organization membership (such as nomination by a current member) by visiting the organization website(s).

4. Consider taking a few business courses so you can learn more about how to start and maintain your travel agency most effectively. Search the course offerings at your local community college and online. Any fees paid to enroll or participate in courses related to the operation of your business are tax deductible.

- You may be able to find training courses specific to running a travel agency.
- Even if you have previous business education or experience, a refresher course can be very helpful, especially for learning up-to-date laws.

5. Promote your business. This can be done in a number of ways and should depend at least in part upon your target demographic and their consumer habits. However, much of modern marketing is online, and this is where you should start as a home-based travel agent -- especially since the majority of your business will likely be conducted online.

- Use social media! Create a profile page on LinkedIn, Facebook, Instagram, Twitter, or some other widely-used social media site. Post often about offers and services. This should help you attract business through visual exposure.
- Create a channel on YouTube or Vimeo and showcase destinations or resorts with whom your customers have recently booked. You can link the videos to your social media accounts.

6. Establish a customer incentive program. In order to get more business via word-of-mouth, offer rewards to clients who refer additional customers to you. These can be in the form of a simple voucher for discounted future services, gift certificates to local restaurants or stores, or just about anything else you choose.

- If you aren't sure what sorts of incentives your customers are most likely to be interested in, offer a range of rewards for successful referrals. You can also survey customers to discover majority preferences and use this to design your incentive program.
- If you can figure out an incentive system early enough, incorporate this into your business plan.

How to Be a Travel Agent

Many people are attracted to a career as a travel agent because of the perks: discounts on lodging, transportation, and constant opportunities to see the world. They offer advice on travel, put together travel packages, research vacation spots and confirm arrangements. To be a travel agent, determine the skills you need, take advantage of educational opportunities and professional resources, and consider specializing in a particular type of travel.

Part 1

Education and Training

1. Get a high school diploma. Typical for any job nowadays, a high school diploma is necessary to get started. This is the bare minimum for entry into an established business.

- A GED is fine. Whichever form you choose, it's essential to get good grades and to learn computer skills.

2. Take classes in travel planning. Having extra, focused knowledge makes you a prime candidate when you walk into any office (or start your own business).

- Check out your local community colleges, vocational schools, and industry associations for classes. The classes should focus on reservation systems, travel regulations (both domestic and international), and marketing.

3. Get a degree in travel and tourism. Few schools offer on-site degrees in this, but it's worth the research if one is in your area. However, loads offer classes online.

- University of Southern Mississippi
- Johnson & Wales University
- University of Massachusetts Isenberg School of Management
- East Carolina University
- Robert Morris University
- Strayer University
- If you plan to start your own travel agency, you will need business courses as well.

4. Get a business license. Depending on your location and business set-up, you may need a travel agent license (if you have a host, you may be able to use their license number). Even if you don't live in an area that requires one but are planning to sell to residents of those states, it's worth looking into.

- 6 US states currently have seller of travel laws:
    - California (the strictest and most complex)
    - Florida
    - Iowa
    - Washington
    - Hawaii
    - Nevada (suspended until July 2013)
- Louisiana and Delaware have loose restrictions on new agencies.
- All agents and supervisors/managers in Ontario, Canada must take the Travel Industry Council of Ontario (TICO) exam. It currently rings up at $32 CAD.
- Travel agencies in British Columbia, Canada are required by the Insurance Council of British Columbia to take a travel insurance exam. It's a license tied to the agency and every travel agent in the agency is required to attend 2 hours of training a year.
- The licensing for those in Saskatchewan, Canada is again related to travel insurance and involves an exam required by the Insurance Council of Saskatchewan. Unlike the licensing in British Columbia though, this license is tied to the travel agent, not the agency. Agents are required to attend 3 hours of training every year.

5. Get credentials. These generally take two forms; both add to your credibility as a travel agent.

- Classes and training at an undergrad level and your IATAN (International Airlines Travel Agent Network) ID card.
- Supplemental training at schools like The Travel Institute and the International Airline Transport Association's Training and Development Institute. Both provide training and professional development opportunities for *experienced* travel agents. Examinations for different levels of certification are offered depending on a travel agent's experience.
- If you have a designated area of interest, certification from an organization such as the Cruise Lines International Association could never hurt.
- Beware of "card-mills." For a relatively small fee, they mysteriously give you a "travel agent qualification." It's a scam.

Part 2

Skills and Know-how

1. Develop the personality. To be a successful travel agent, you must be worldly, confident, and one heck of a networker. Even if you're working for a parent company, you have to convince your clients that you're offering them the best vacation they could possibly have.

- Be adventurous. Part of the job description is willing to scope out and analyze different, sometimes dangerous, sometimes exotic, areas.
- Hone your communication skills. When you're not doing on-the-scene research, you'll be behind a desk, emailing and talking on the phone. Your success rate is based on how well you can communicate.
- Zero-in on the details. Every person has a different ideal vacation—making sure everything from the curtains to the bus air conditioning system is beyond the standard is what makes a returning customer.
- Get organized. You'll be dealing with dozens of itineraries simultaneously. Keeping things straight and meeting deadlines is imperative to success.
- Make connections. You're going to need clients to make commission, so start talking. Be the go-to for all your friends and family when it comes to travel information and itinerary organization. Start networking today.

2. Be well-traveled. You cannot sell a product that you're unfamiliar with. Getting out there or seeing it for yourself puts you in the clients' shoes and prepares you for unforeseen problems.

- Being able to dispense first-hand information is invaluable. Clients are more interested in hearing suggestions based on first-hand accounts of services, accommodations and geographic areas. This is the reason travel agents often receive discounts while traveling.
- Knowing a foreign language (or two) definitely helps!

3. Know the facts. Before you start any career, familiarize yourself with the market and what you're getting into.

- The beginning travel agent makes, on average, around $15 an hour or around $30,000 a year.
- In the US as of 2010, there were 82,000 travel agents (a 10% rise is projected for 2020).

4. Become a destination specialist. In order to thrive in this work environment, it's helpful to have an area of expertise. Have you wandered the markets of Istanbul? Cracked coconuts in the Mekong Delta? Choose a region that appeals to you.

- Some specialties could include a specific geographic location like Mexico; specific types of travel like cruises or tour groups; price-focused travel such as luxury accommodations or affordable vacations; and particular travel groups based on hobbies, special interests or lifestyles such as seniors or vegetarians.

5. Pick your work environment. The number of travel agents working for themselves is increasing rapidly. Decide whether you want to work under the umbrella of a brick and mortar company or just through a host company, working on your own.

- YTB, Traverse, and GT Trends all give you a website that you call "your own" for a minimal fee. They train and support you and provide your initial income. They all have a parent company; if you'd like to cut out the middleman, you can pair with the parent company yourself. As always, do the research yourself to find what's right for you.

Part 3

On the Job

1. Apply for a job in a travel agency. Starting as a receptionist or assistant can lead to more responsibilities and opportunities to advance while you're enrolled in a travel agent program.

- Don't be afraid to just get your foot in the door. Some companies, like Virtuoso, recommend 20 years of experience before you start working with them.

2. Start networking. Whether you're working from home or in an office, raising your voice is the only way to let people know you're getting on the ground and running. Do the research and start making offers.

- Create a referral service with another travel agent or agents who can refer business to you in your specialty and you can do the same for them. You can sometimes work out a mutual-referral agreement with another agent in order to collect referral fees.

3. Join an organization. The quickest way to hone your craft is to observe and mirror other profes-

sionals in your field. Join an organization to surround yourself with similar individuals who may be a few years ahead of you.

- Professional organizations, such as the American Society of Travel Agents (ASTA) provide support, further education and training opportunities, resources, networking opportunities, travel tools, publication access, evaluation services, invitations to seminars, expos and summits, scholarships for students and salary tools.
- These organizations also give you access to job boards and travel school directories, if you're looking for career rejuvenation.

How to Become a Travel Agent Online

Being an online travel agent has become a popular stay-at-home job over the years. There are numerous Internet travel agencies that offer training, certifications and the opportunity to start your own travel agency. With so much competition to face online, a smart tactic is to specialize in certain types of travel or destinations so you can market yourself as an expert. Before you start your very own agency, however, it is recommended that you start your career as an independent contractor for an established host agency so you can learn the ins and outs with minimal startup costs and less financial risk.

Part 1

Determining your Specialty in the Travel Market

1. Consider what sort of travel agent you wish to be. Resist the urge to instantly become a travel agent for all people interested in all destinations. Due to the limitless competition you will face on the internet, aim to be a sought-after expert, rather than a jack-of-all-trades. Just as a restaurateur must settle on a cuisine, menu, and customer demographic, start thinking about what sort of packages and destinations you would like to offer to which sort of people.

- Two distinct types of travel agents are "corporate" and "leisure" agents. The former makes arrangements for companies whose personnel who must travel for their work. The latter books personal vacations for individuals.

- Leisure agents may specialize in terms of themes (such as adventure or romantic getaways), destinations (with a thorough knowledge and plenty of advice for their customers), or clientele (catering to those traveling on a budget or those with unlimited means).

2. Write down your interests. Increase your passion for the job and your chances of success by focusing on areas that already fascinate you. First, jot down your interests in general terms, even if they seem to have nothing to do with travel. Then create a second list of destinations that you loved visiting or would love to go to. Compare the two lists. Try to pair your interests with specific destinations that pertain to them to double your enthusiasm. For example:

- If fine wine is on your list of interests, pair it with areas on your list of destinations that include wine countries, such as France, Italy, or California.
- London would be an area to focus on if you have a passion for English literature.
- If you are obsessed with great white sharks, think about Australia, Baja, and South Africa.

3. Determine your client base. Imagine yourself back in the role of travel agent. Now picture who you would most like to see going off on your dream vacation in your place. Consider not just the destination, but the nature of your dream travel package. Perhaps most importantly, consider how much money you envision your ideal customers spending.

- Contact other travel agents for quotes to get a rough idea of the going price for the sort of dream trips you would like to offer your own clients.
- Use this price information to determine what sort of income your clients would need to afford these trips.

- Factor in any age restrictions that may further narrow your potential client list down. A wine-tasting tour, for example, would most likely eliminate families traveling with children, while cage-diving with sharks might appeal more to younger adults than senior citizens.

Part 2

Laying the Groundwork for your Business

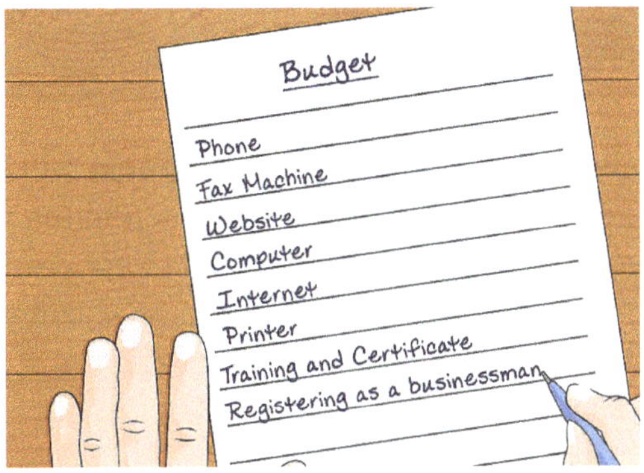

1. Create a budget. Set aside money to cover essential equipment for an online business. These items include a phone, a fax machine, a website, and a computer with Internet access and a printer. Also anticipate having to possibly pay fees for the following:

- Training and certification
- Registering as a business

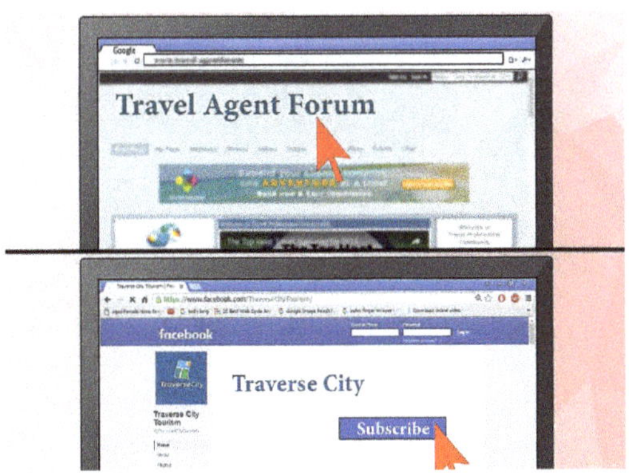

2. Use available resources to learn about the industry. If you know anyone who works as a travel agent, treat them to a cup of coffee so you can pick their brain. Visit online forums and message boards that are specific to the industry to see what issues insiders talk about. Join professional networks. Subscribe to publications that are dedicated to the business.

- GT Trends, Traverse, and YTP Travel Network are prominent professional networks in the industry.
- Trade-specific publications include Agent@Home, Recommend, Travolution, Travel Agent Central, and Travel Trade.

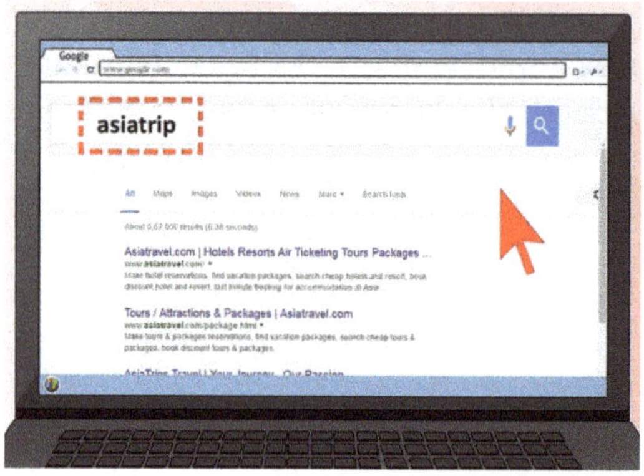

3. Come up with a name for your business. Since your business will be based online, keep it short so people can remember and search for it easily. Google each name you think of to see if that specific domain name has already been taken and/or if that exact company name has already been registered by another entity. Also take note of the top hits that come up with each search. Even if the name you want is currently free, consider something different if your website is likely to come 50th in a list of other popular searches.

- For example, let's say that you personally share the same name as Donald Trump. Since a Google search will bury any mention of you online under a million other sites regarding the Don, come up with a business name that does not incorporate your own name in any way.
- Including the core concept of your speciality in your business name can increase its prominence in keyword searches for those terms. For example, "California Wine Tours" is self-explanatory as well as being the exact phrase someone would Google to find more information about that topic.

4. Register your business. Consult a lawyer and/or tax accountant about which classification best suits your business: sole proprietor, partnership, LLC, or corporation. As a small business, you will most likely register as a sole proprietor. In that event, ask your lawyer if local or state laws require you to register a "Doing Business As" (DBA) name with those governments.

- Such registrations as DBA's are often what is meant by a "travel agent license." In this sense of the word "license," you are essentially paying a nominal fee and filling out some paperwork in order to work from a residence, as opposed to taking classes and passing exams in order to earn a driver's license.

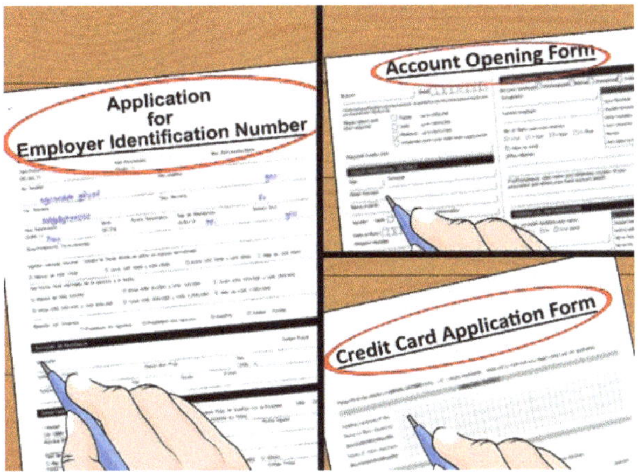

5. Separate your personal and business finances. Apply for an Employer Identification Number (EIN) to use for tax purposes in lieu of your Social Security number. Open a bank account specifically for your business to keep better track of company expenses. If your business needs a credit card in addition to the debit card that comes with your new bank account, apply for a new credit card to be used exclusively for your company.

- These steps are not strictly necessary to start your business, but will help keep you organized.

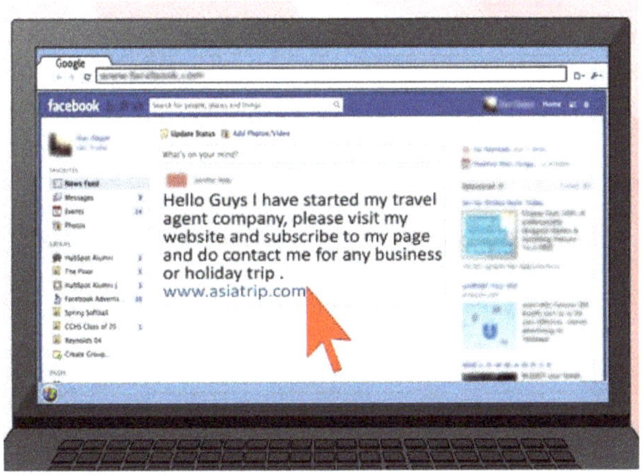

6. Utilize your contacts. Review the people in your life. Consider all categories: family, friends, friends of friends, neighbors, classmates, co-workers, passing acquaintances. Ask yourself if there is anyway they can help promote or otherwise assist your business. For example, if you would like to specialize in wine-tasting tours to the Napa Valley and your neighbor's son works at a hotel there, ask for his contact information. Or if you plan to arrange group trips to major sporting events, keep the diehard sports fans in your life in mind as possible links to future customers.

- Use social media like Facebook and Twitter to link your business to your existing contacts. Increase your visibility. Ask them to like your website and share your posts so others in their network see you in their own feeds.
- Ask people you know to refer potential customers to you. Encourage them by offering prizes or thank-you gifts for referrals who end up booking trips with you.

Part 3

Joining a Host Agency

1. Consider signing up up with a host agency. Although you are free to start an online travel agency that is totally independent of any other business entity, consider starting as an independent contractor for a host agency instead. Transition into your new career with less stress by utilizing their pre-existing infrastructure. Learn the trade and gain insight into what is needed to construct your own successful business before attempting to start one from scratch. Host agencies will provide:

- Training
- Community support
- Lower overhead

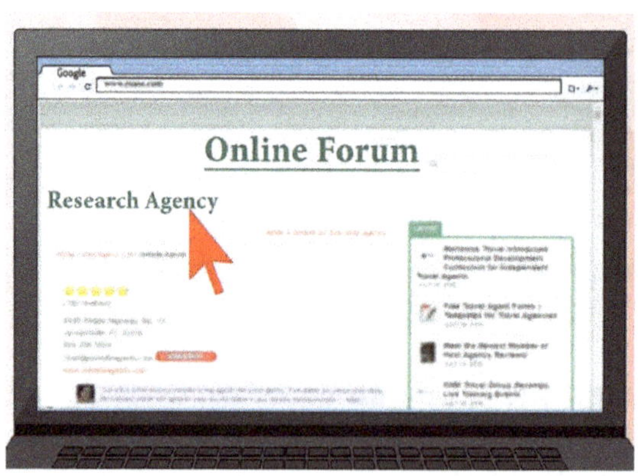

2. Research agencies. There are numerous host agencies out there, so take the time to familiarize yourself with any given one before applying to join. Read customer reviews to see if the company's brand is sought after by the public or avoided at all costs. Visit forums frequented by current and former agents who worked with them to find out what sort of experiences they had. Call each agency to discuss information that may not have mentioned on their website. Ask about:

- What sort of commission they offer and the method of payment.
- Which software programs you will need and whether they offer a discount if you purchase the tech through them instead of the open market.

- The amount of training that is required and what amount of continued education is offered after that.
- What sort of community support is offered between you, other independent contractors, and the agency itself.
- Exactly how much you will be charged to sign up, as well as any fees that may be required later on.

3. Determine which is best suited for you. Once you have made contact with agencies and familiarized yourself with their operations, weigh their answers to your questions against your own personal needs. First and foremost, consider those that already offer travel within the niche market that you have decided to specialize in. Additionally, ask yourself the following:

- Would you rather work for a large company with extensive resources, or a smaller one with DIY spirit and more intimate connections between workers?
- Are you fine working remotely with people you will never meet, or would you rather work for a local business that occasionally gets together?
- Does the training that they offer seem to cover everything you need to learn, or do you feel that you will still be overwhelmed afterward?

4. Sign up with the agency. The process for each agency will vary, but expect to pay an application fee. If they offer a training and certification course, the application fee may cover these, or they

may be billed separately. Complete the coursework assigned in the specified amount of time to receive certification.

- Courses may be designed to be entirely online, by correspondence, or a combination of the two.
- Certification is not a legal requirement to be a travel agent, so if the host agency does not offer their own certification process, you can still apply and possibly be hired. If you wish to work for this specific company and boast about being certified at the same time, you can seek certification through organizations like the Travel Institute.

How to Make your Own Travel Portal

A travel portal is an online gateway that helps readers online find our more information about the travel agency of company whose site it is, using an attractive and simplified method.

Steps

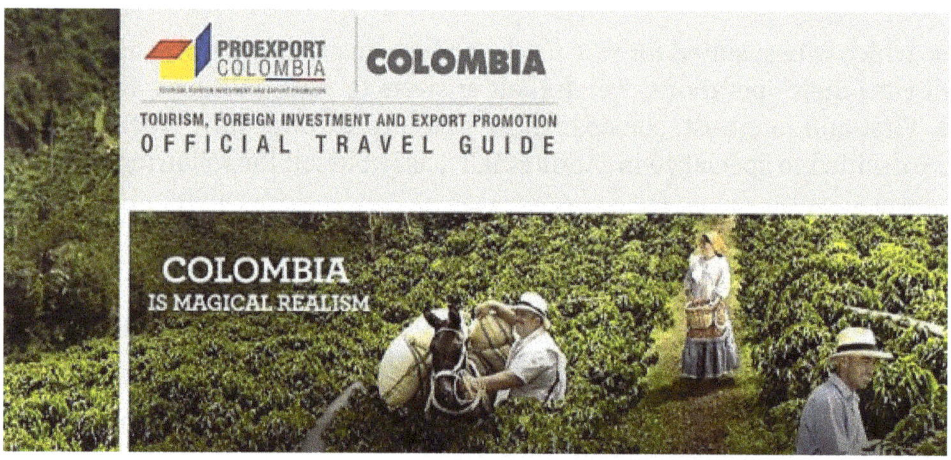

1. Design a travel portal which is striking. Make the front page attractive, using a few pictures of the various destinations you, as a travel agent, deal with. Avoid overcrowding it with images, as this will confuse readers and can increase site opening time, making users irritated.

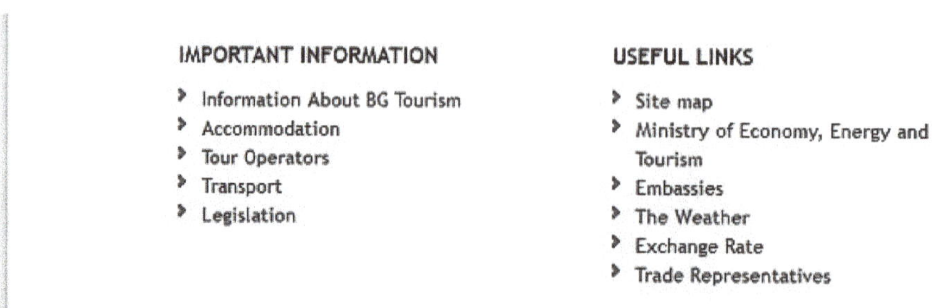

2. Try to provide the index of all contents that can be found on other pages of the website. This will help simplify the work of the hopeful traveler.

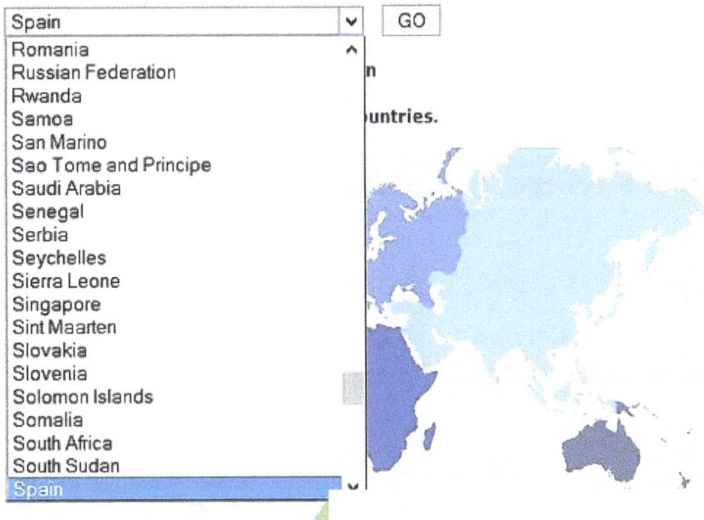

3. Provide the information of all the destinations in short form. The travel portal must be informative enough about the destination readers are looking for. Provide brief information about the location, climate, best time to visit, food and other stuff relevant to each place. The best option to attract people is to tell about the main attractions of each place are and how they can visit them.

4. Provide the users with information about any discounts and deals.

5. Provide readers with various options for doing things after reaching their destination. This helps the user enjoy their own planning freedom, as apart from receiving their accommodation booked from the agent, they can opt for various travel guides that may help them when they get there. This can fetch your agency extra money, as well as increasing your good reputation.

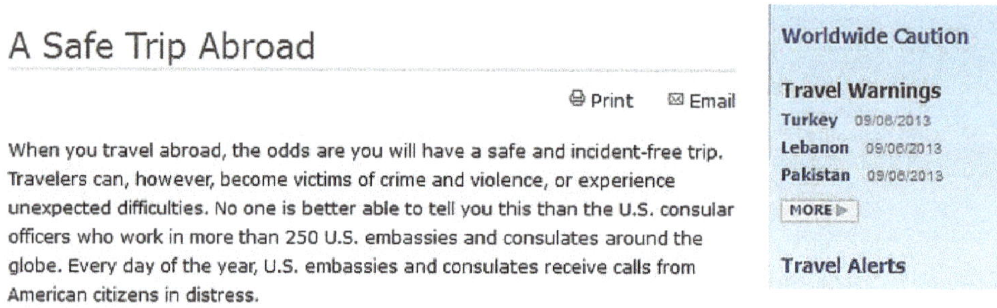

6. Provide information about safety and precautions. Explain also how your company provides security; doing this can create reassurance for users.

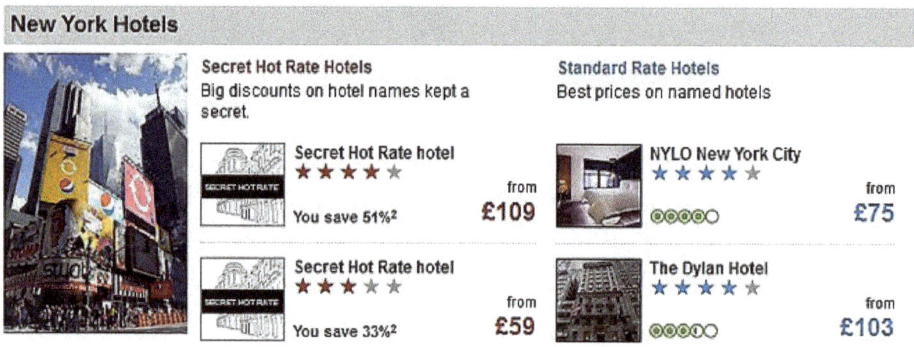

7. Add links from each page to the others. Don't make readers do all the hard work.

8. Post the various feedback and testimonials of happy customer. Doing this can attract lot of users, as it will be a kind of recommendation of your website. Don't hold back from explaining how you have successfully dealt with complaints, either, as this will build a sense of trust in your ability to be responsive to customers.

How to Make a Travel Brochure

A creative, expertly written and well-designed travel brochure invites readers to cast themselves into a story that takes place in an exotic locale. In this topic, learn how to make an enticing travel brochure that will have your audience fantasizing about-and booking-your travel packages.

Part 1

Determining the Details of your Travel Brochure

1. Choose the destination of your potential clients. If you are a professional working for a travel company, your destination of choice will be the one you work for. If you are a student, and are creating a pretend travel brochure, you will want to pick out a desirable, exotic, and interesting location.

- A professional should already know what destination he/she is representing, or attempting to advertise for. Use this step to get to know the key features of your location: mountains, lakes, cabins, museums, parks, etc. Write each of these key features down on a piece of paper for use later on.
- If you are a student, find some place exciting to advertise for. Some great examples are Mexico, Hawaii, Myrtle Beach South Carolina, the beaches of Florida, or Australia to name a few. Research the location you choose (using online search engines, encyclopedias, library books, etc.) and find out key features about the location. Write each of these down on a piece of paper for use later on.
- The lists for both students and professionals should be extra long at the beginning. It is better to create a long list to start, and then cross off items later on.

2. Explore and locate the amenities of the location. These include, but are not limited to, restaurants, shops, bathrooms, movie theaters, etc. It is important that your potential client knows what the amenities are, and where they are located at your destination.

- Travel around the site by yourself and write down what and where the particular amenity is.
- If you are far away from where you are advertising for, look for maps online that might help you locate particular amenities. Sites like Google Maps point out exactly what and where each of these is.
- After you have created a detailed list of the amenities, put a star next to the items you think are most important (bathrooms generally are a top priority). Make sure to note whether these amenities provide accommodations such as whether they are handicap accessible.

3. Find out what the residents are saying. If you live with, or near, persons whom live there, talk to them. Get their opinions/first hand accounts of what the destination is like.

- Visit peoples' homes and ask them to give their opinion. Remember to bring a pencil and paper to write down exactly what they say. You can also bring a voice recorder if you do not write very fast.
- If the destination is strictly for vacation (non-residential) try calling people whom have vacationed there in the past. As with the previous step, write down exactly what they have to say about their experience.
- Students who do not have direct contact with persons whom live, or have vacationed there, should look online. Find internet sites that link you with local hotels, restaurants, etc. in the area of your destination. Look for reviews that have to do with the *destination* (Mexico, Hawaii, etc.) rather than a particular place of accommodation. Write down what they have to say.

4. Pick your target audience. For every destination, you will need to figure out what demographic

group will be most interested. This will not only help you highlight particular accommodations, but also create a brochure that is visually stimulating to your targeted demographic group.

- Use your list of key features and amenities to pick a target audience. Here are some key examples which will help:
    - Vacation spots with lots of bathrooms, and restaurants available are great for an older demographic audience.
    - Destinations which are primarily vacation spots (non-residential) usually target a younger audience, or newlywed couples on their honeymoon.
    - Vacation spots which have hotels furnished with wifi and cable are great to bring your kids too.
    - Destinations which have large rooms are great for business types, looking to conduct work from far away.
- This is not an all encompassing list, but it will give you an idea about what to look for, and how to pick the right demographic audience. Something you might think is minor (board-walk for example) might make all the difference in the world for a particular clientele.

5. Determine the price of your travel package. This is the most important step of all. You need to make a reasonable profit, but you also do not want to scare away potential visitors. If you are a professional, the price of the trip will probably already be determined.

- Take into account the previous four steps, and in particular the target demographic group. Set a standard price to each of the amenities, and add them all up. Set a standard price for all of the key features of the destination and add them all up. Finally, add the price of the amenities and destination hot-spots together.
- Adjust the vacation cost according to who the audience is. Younger clientele, and families will most likely be looking for a cheaper vacation. Older clientele, and business types will have more money to spend. Generally speaking, vacations for a family of four should run between $1000 and $2000. Go higher or lower as you see fit.

Part 2

Writing the Text of your Travel Brochure

1. Create a preliminary outline. Before you begin to publish a final copy, you will want to practice writing exactly what you want to say in the brochure. This is a great time to check spelling, grammar, and punctuation.

- First you want to create a story. Just like a good novel pulls in a reader, the client wants to feel as if he or she is going on an adventure. In paragraph form (full sentences) write a convincing argument for why the vacation spot is the best place to visit.
- After you have written down your argument, go back and check for edits. More importantly, cross out extraneous information, keep what is critical, and add in to places that need a more exciting, or convincing argument.
- This argument can then be split apart into different sections of your brochure. You might have to tailor the sentences to exist as a stand-alone argument in the different sections, but this will give you a good head start. It is important that the writer knows exactly why each of the individual pieces are critical, and how they come together to convince the clientele.

2. Use specialized fonts and lettering. The brochure should be legible, and easy to follow. There should be an overall flow to the brochure, and not feel discombobulated.

- Your heading/title should appear in bold lettering, underlined, and be large enough to read from far away. If someone is sitting in a doctors office, or at a coffee shop, they should be able to see the title clearly, at the top of the brochure.
- Each of the subheadings/section headings should also be in bold, and underlined. They should be a slightly smaller font size than the title. They should all also all be the same font. If one subtitle is in Times New Roman, keep them all Times New Roman. This creates a nice flow to your brochure, and does not bog down the viewer in trying to comprehend the brochure.

3. Write a captivating title. Simple tag lines like "Mexican Vacation" or "Hawaiian Vacation" are going to bore the potential vacationers and not draw them in to read the rest of the brochure. You need to use descriptive adjectives, possibly even verbs, to entice the viewer.

- Write down some adjectives you know that are not typically used, such as adventurous, pulsating, mind-boggling, fanciful, breathtaking, etc. Put these words first in your title, so that the readers eyes, reading left to right, will catch that key word.
- Then make sure to include the location in the title. If you advertising for a Hawaiian vacation, do not leave out the word Hawaii. Put the location right after the adjective.
- Following the name of the place, you can finish the title with simply "vacation" or a synonym. End the title in an exclamation point, so that it appears that the person selling the vacation is just as excited as the potential clientele.
- Bold the lettering, and underline the title. Example: Adventurous Mount Everest Vacation.

4. Hook your audience with the opening sentence. This sentence should appear on the first flap the reader opens up to. Think of this sentence as a thesis statement of a paper.

- You want to make clear the argument for this vacation right up front. The reader is not going to look around the rest of the brochure, if he or she is not convinced at the very beginning.
- This would be a great time to simply list off a few of the accommodations/hot spots. For example: An all-encompassing Hawaiian vacation that includes beautiful scenery, top-of-the-line hotels, and all the food you can eat.

5. Write each of your sections. Your brochure is going to be about half visuals, and half written words. So for each section of the brochure, you will only use a few sentences (3-4) to explain each distinct aspect of the vacation.

- You will want to include, at the bare minimum, the following sections: restaurants, hotels, scenery(appearance of the vacation spot), and shops. These are four of the most basic things people need to know about before they go on the vacation. In total, you should have around six to eight sections.
- Make sure that what you are saying is necessary, succinct, and convincing. Consider what image you are using and make sure that the words match up. Feel free to highlight, italicize, or bold certain words or phrases.
- This would also be a great time to add in those accommodations, such as handicap accessible, free continental breakfast, bike/walking trails, etc.

6. Copy and edit testimonials. Earlier you gathered and wrote down the personal experiences of

people whom have previously been on vacation there. This is a great time to not only include a summary of what they said, but include block quotes.

- To include block quotes in your brochure, start by indenting. Then add a quotation mark, and write in your quote. Finish by adding another quotation mark.
- You will want to include only the most sensitive, valuable information. Do not include bad experiences, as this might turn off the clientele.
- If you want to take out a sentence in the middle of a paragraph, simply highlight and delete. Then, in between the remaining sentences, add (three periods in a row). This will allow you to shorten the quote, keep what is necessary, and highlight what is most important.

7. Include a price section. This is not an all encompassing section. There is no need to create a chart, showing them all the options. However, you should give them a ballpark figure as to how much the vacation should cost.

- Include, in your 3-4 sentence price section, some simple terms, such as: Prices as low as $1000 for a family of four! or, Prices start at $1500, and include great discounts if you purchase by phone.
- Mention the different offers/deals vacationers can get through your particular company. Usually there are family discounts, senior discounts, children discounts, etc.
- This section should appear on the inside of the pamphlet, to the far right (at the end). You do not want to start the brochure by introducing price. Nor do you want to put the price on the back of the brochure, as the clientele will probably look there first and never look inside.

8. Link the viewer to other sources. This is critical because the brochure will not be enough. After

the price section, or on the back of the brochure, include a section that links email addresses, web page addresses, phone numbers, and a mailing address.

- This should be done as a series of bulleted points, or dashes. Do not write this information in paragraph form, as it will all run together.
- Check a second and third time that the information is up to date and correct. Look at the bottom of webpages to see when the last time the page was updated. Call the numbers you are listing on the brochure and see who picks up the phone. The information you are presenting needs to be accurate.

Part 3

Creating the Visuals for your Travel Brochure

1. Choose eye-catching photos. These photos will help you tell the story you want to tell. The clientele should be excited and intrigued by what they see in the brochure.

- Examples: A smiling visitor hugging a dolphin at a sea life attraction, or a woman relaxing with a massage in an open-air spa that overlooks the tropical sunset.
- Make sure the photos are in color, and have a high-quality resolution. Do not use stock photos which generally look fake, and off-putting. Use real life images, or photos you have taken yourself at the location.
- People enjoy seeing others having fun, so try to include photos of people enjoying themselves at your destination rather than showing an empty hotel room or deserted beach. This will invite readers to project themselves into the photo.

2. Consider the color scheme carefully. Each vacation will have a different feel/tone. You will want to convey whether your destination is relaxing, exciting, or somewhere in between.

- To convey a relaxed feeling appropriate for a spa, use muted pastel tones. Children's destinations are best marketed with bright, bold colors. Historical site brochures can be given an "antique" feeling with sepia and earth tones.
- For each panel of the brochure, use the same color. If there are different colors for each panel, it can become distracting and gaudy.

3. Add in borders, asterisks, and designs. While you never want to distract the viewer too much, these three things can help in the aid of the story you are trying to tell.

- Use a thin border to contain each of the panels in your brochure. A thick border can become distracting. The border should be a color that is a slightly darker/lighter shade of the tone that you use for the rest of the brochure.
- If you want to highlight key points of your story, use bullet points or asterisks. Generally, 3-4 is the range you want to stay in. Try to highlight things that are not written about in the sentences.
- Designs can also help, such as stars, rainbows, arrows, etc. Add these where and when you see fit. Once more, do not overuse these, and bog down the viewer in the visuals. The clientele should want to read more, not necessarily look more.

4. Organize the brochure so the copy and visuals work together. The 3-4 sentence sections should match what the visuals are saying. Example: If you are talking about restaurants in your section, use a picture of a restaurant.

5. Invest in a professional printing company. If you are a student, a standard folded piece of paper will work just fine. However, professionals should look at printing brochures at facilities that specialize in printing.

- Tell the printing company that you want the brochures printed on high-quality paper. Cheap, flimsy paper can easily be torn, ripped, or water-damaged. Thick, coated paper provides resistance to accidents, and can be carried around mush easier.
- If you wind up using your home or business printer, just make sure to use thick, heavy paper. The settings of your printer should be set to the highest pixel quality so that your pictures come out clean and crisp.

6. Provide a final copy proof. Make sure the printing company has not dramatically changed/altered the layout or design of the brochure. For both professionals and students, this is a great time to go back and spell/grammar check one more time.

How to Create a Travel Itinerary

A travel itinerary outlines all elements of a trip, from hotel stops to destinations. It can be indispensable, whether you're planning a weekend vacation or an extended road trip. A good itinerary gives a trip structure, and maximizes the amount you'll be able to see and do. Though it seems a daunting task, an itinerary is simple to develop. With your basic travel information and a map, you can plan an entire trip out in an efficient and organized manner.

Part 1

Planning and Mapping your Itinerary

1. Collect the important information for your trip. Flight numbers, hotels, car rentals, and restaurant reservations are all key pieces of information to manage and maintain. You may also want to include directions to your hotel, the car rental company you are using, as well as directions to the airport for your return flight. If you will be using airport transportation to get to your hotel, include information about fees and hours of operation.

2. Make a list. It's helpful to list all of the things you want to do on your trip. Even if it's more than you think you can manage, create a list of everything you'd like to do. Research local events, holidays, and observances of the places you're traveling too as well. You may be able to witness or experience a cultural event that other travelers don't get to experience.

- Be conscious of the amount of time you will spend at each stop. Certain destinations, like the Museum of Modern Art, can be an all-day endeavor.
- If you're traveling with one or more people, be sure to get feedback and ideas for your destinations.

3. Map your stops. Match your stops to specific locations on a map and note their locations. Try and map them sequentially to efficiently use your travel time. You'll most likely be traveling from adjacent cities as you travel. For each activity, estimate the length of time it will take to get to there, and how long you will be there.

- Be sure you have local maps for the areas you will be exploring. It is also helpful to obtain schedules for bus and train services and numbers for local taxis.

4. Create a budget. Do you want a trip with days spent at four star restaurants and nights spent in five star hotels? Or are you more interested in finding local favorites and rustic B&Bs? Your vacation is as expensive (or inexpensive) as you want it to be. It ultimately comes down to what you can afford.

- A spreadsheet program like Microsoft Excel can help create an organized and portable budget and itinerary.

5. Stay flexible. Don't hesitate to give yourself a free day or two. You can use this free day to ex-

plore, or take some time off to rest. Ultimately your itinerary is a guide to keep you on track while visiting. If you miss a reservation, it isn't the end of the world. Consider asking around about a local favorite to eat at, find a local market, or see if there's a museum or oddity nearby. Never lose sight of the fact that your trip is supposed to be an enjoyable and fulfilling experience.

Part 2

Organizing your Itinerary

1. Record your information. Record your check in times, confirmation numbers, hotel names, and any other information you might need on hand. Don't worry about organizing this information yet. In the meantime, focus on accumulating and documenting as much helpful information as you can think of.

2. Organize your travel information. Try and condense your travel information into a single document for easy access while traveling. Keep a printed copy or type the details of your itinerary into a word processing document. If you prefer, you can use an online travel itinerary template.

- You may also consider downloading a travel app to keep organized during your trip.

3. Keep a hard-copy. Your travel itinerary can be placed into a 3-ring binder. As convenient as an app can be, batteries can die. It never hurts to keep a physical backup handy. Use page dividers to separate documents in your trip binder into categories (rental car, tours, hotel reservations, etc.).

4. Create a database. Compile a print-out or Notepad note of information for your emergency contact(s) back home, and any special medical needs you or your travel companions may have. If you are traveling out of the country, include the address, telephone number, and directions to your country's embassy or consulate if applicable.

- You may want to save a list of addresses of family and friends, so you can send them post-cards from the destinations you will visit.

5. Account for your responsibilities. Even if you will only be gone for a weekend, it's a good idea to

make sure that everything at home will be in order and accounted for. If you have pets, plants, or will need your mail checked for an extended amount of time, ensure that a friend or family member will be there to do so. This will ultimately offer you peace of mind so you can relax and fully enjoy your vacation.

CHAPTER 2 Methods of Budget Travel

Traveling on a budget requires careful planning and consideration must be given about food and drink, lodging and duration. Budget travel has limitations but it is an upcoming trend to visit another region or go on a holiday without spending a lot of money. Budget travel is best understood in confluence with the major topics listed in the following chapter.

How to Calculate Cost of Travel

Any time you plan a trip, it is helpful to know how much it will cost to travel to and from your destination. Several factors must be taken into consideration in order to get an accurate figure for the amount of money a trip will cost. Follow these steps to calculate cost of travel.

Steps

1. Calculate the cost of transportation. Transportation is likely to be 1 of the biggest travel costs you will incur. If you are taking a plane, train or bus, then your transportation cost equates to the price of your ticket. If you are driving, you will need to calculate the cost of the rental vehicle, if applicable, and the amount of gas your trip will require. This is mostly aimed at cost per US or CAN Dollar, for UK Pound / Euro Dollar you may have to adjust manually.

- Start with the distance you will be driving, in miles or kilometers.
- Divide the distance by your car's fuel economy (miles per gallon or kilometers per liter). The resulting amount is the number of gallons or liters it will take you to complete your trip.
- Multiply the number of gallons or liters by the average cost of fuel.

- Note: If you drive a rental vehicle, the rental company will charge you a fixed amount per mile and, additionally, a fixed amount for car insurance. Be sure to factor these amounts into your travel costs.

2. Include all costs that are incurred while traveling.

- Food and drink - If you travel for an extended period of time, you will need to stop for food and drink, or you may opt to pack food and drink. Either way, you must include this expense in your cost of travel calculation.
- Lodging - For trips that require driving for more than 1 day, you will need to stop over somewhere to get some sleep. Unless you opt to pull to the side of the road and sleep in your vehicle, you will need to add the cost of lodging to your overall travel costs.
- Tolls - Many road routes have a series of toll booths that you must stop at as you travel. The cost of tolls can add up, especially if you are on a long road trip.
- Parking - If you opt to take a plane, train or bus, then you may need to add the cost of storing your automobile in a parking lot or garage to your travel costs.
- Depreciation - Any time you drive your vehicle, the value of your vehicle depreciates, and that figure must be added to your cost of travel calculation. Depreciation can be figured by multiplying the average cost of depreciation, 27 cents per 1 mile (5 cents per 1.6 km), by the distance you will be traveling.
- Indirect costs - Indirect travel costs should be considered if you are driving, and include things like road maintenance, pollution, government taxes, accidents and land use. To calculate indirect costs, multiply .05 cents by the number of miles or .01 cents by the number of kilometers you will be driving.
- Time to travel - Also consider your time on the road vs. destination if you're going on vacation; to calculate this take the hours it will take to travel to your destination, add each stop point time (food, restroom, refuel) per 15min increments, and you will have a total time to get to your destination. If you want to figure out how much 'money' you have lost in your delays (an average time vs. pay for your job if you're traveling for such a reason) take the

amount you're getting paid total to arrive on time and subtract 10 cents for every 5 min you are not traveling, this will give you an average cost of what you will lose or gain for being on time.

3. If you have to, consider time taken off work. When figuring the cost to travel, the time you miss from work must be added to the equation. Take the number of hours you will be missing and multiply that by the amount of money you make per hour.

How to Create a Travel Budget

Travel is a great way to clear your mind and find memorable experiences. However, travel can be expensive and may require you to save up and budget your costs ahead of time. By taking time to consider your costs thoroughly, both for necessities and for leisure, you will have a working budget ready for your trip.

Part 1

Creating an Initial Budget

1. Determine what you can afford. Assess how much money you have available for the vacation.

Keep in mind your ongoing expenses that you'll need to take care of when you return like rent, utilities, and food costs. You don't want to stress yourself out during your vacation by having no money for when you return.

2. Get advice from friends and family. Ask around if anyone you know has visited your destination. While websites and web reviews are helpful, you don't know if they've been influenced by local sponsors or the like. Friends and family will give you more personal and trustworthy advice.

- Ask questions like "What does a meal cost there?" or "What are some cheap things to do there?"

3. Use online budgeting tools. There are numerous websites designed to help your budget specifically for travel. They will help you determine the local costs of goods and what expenses you'll need to consider.

- Try sites like BudgetYourTrip.com, SavingForTravel.com, and IndepdentTraveler.com. Set up an account and enter the details of your budget and travel expenses.

Part 2

Budgeting for the Basics

1. Determine your method of transportation. Travel to the location of your choosing may be expensive. Determine the costs of taking a plane, train, coach bus, rental car, or cruise ship to your selected location. Air travel is the quickest option but may be costlier than train, bus, or car rental if the distance isn't too great. A cruise ship affords the greatest luxury and will often include a number of stops but is also the costliest option.

- You can compare plane ticket costs with Google Flights, SkyScanner.com, Expedia, FareCompare.com, or Kayak. Always research price comparisons before making your purchase.

2. Consider local transportation. Once you reach your destination, you'll need further transportation to get around locally. Many people take taxi cabs, ride-sharing cars, local transit buses, or the subway to get around locally. If you have some extra money, you can travel more easily by renting a car at your location.

- Use your preferred search engine to research public transit at your destination. Not all cities will have all of the options mentioned above.
- You can compare rental car prices SkyScanner.com, Expedia, or Kayak as well. Always research price comparisons before making your reservation.

- If you are renting a car, you should also consider what rental agencies are close to your airport or hotel.

3. Consider lodging expenses. One of the more significant items you'll need to budget for is your lodging cost. Lodgings vary greatly in cost and quality so be sure to consider your exact needs and what's available at your destination. If your destination hosts many tourists, there will likely be a wide variety of hotels, motels, resorts, and bed-and-breakfasts.

- Pick a hotel that is located near the attractions you're seeking. This will prove convenient and save you in local travel costs.
- Consider amenities like televisions in the rooms, internet access, and access to a swimming pool. You should also consider the quality and size of available beds and bathrooms, the availability of air conditioning, and whether or not they serve a complimentary breakfast. If you have any questions that aren't answered by their website, call the front desk.
- Check customer reviews on Google and Yelp. Keep in mind that nearly every hotel has some excellent reviews and some that are terrible. Read as many as possible to get a comprehensive idea of the quality.
- Some locales will have hostels where you can stay at little or no charge in exchange for doing some chores.
- You can compare hotel prices and features on Expedia and Kayak as well. You can also use Hotwire, Hotels.com, Priceline, Travelocity, and Agoda. Always research price comparisons before making your reservation because different sites may have different prices at the same hotel.

4. Include food costs. Of course, you'll need to eat during your trip so you need to budget for meals.

Keep in mind that you'll likely be eating out and that food costs can vary greatly between different places. Use your preferred search engine to determine local food costs.

- If you need to save some money on food, consider getting a hotel room with a kitchenette or at least a microwave and then purchasing some easy-to-make meals at a local grocery store.

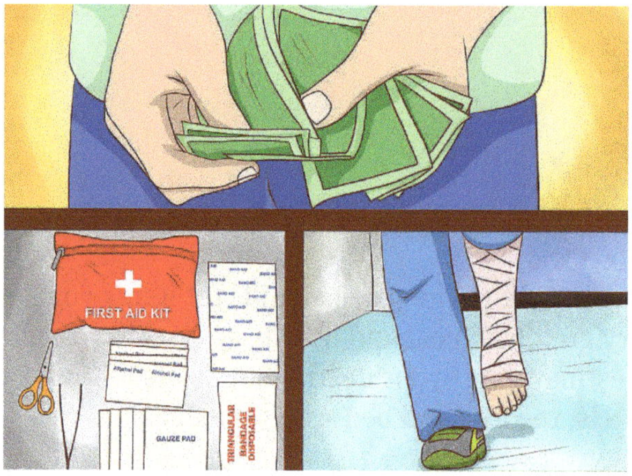

5. Keep an incidentals fund. Always create your travel budget so that there is a little money left over. You're likely to find some sort of cost that you hadn't considered beforehand. It could be as simple as needing sunscreen for the beach or pharmaceuticals for an unforeseen illness.

6. Consider travel insurance. Travel insurance is commonly used to insure against a variety of significant unforeseen costs such as medical care that won't be covered by your insurer because you're out of network, lost luggage, falling victim to theft, or a transportation accident. Travel insurance can often be purchased from vending machines at airports or online.

- Allianz, World Nomads, Travel Guard, and InsureMyTrip are some websites that offer standalone travel insurance.
- You can also get travel insurance from general insurance providers like Geico and State Farm. You may be able to get a discount if you purchase auto, life, or home insurance from these providers already.

Part 3

Budgeting for the Extras

1. Determine sight-seeing costs. Sight-seeing is a common practice for travelers. Think about the transportation, admittance and other costs related specifically to these trips. Most monuments, parks, and museums are free of charge but some may cost a small amount money. Research these sights beforehand so you can factor them into your budget.

- Look up pre-packaged sight-seeing tours in your destination. They may be the most cost-efficient and thorough way to see a locale's major sights.

2. Determine your entertainment costs. If you're planning on attending amusement parks, enjoying the local nightlife, or taking in a show, factor these costs into your budget. You may want to create a rough schedule of your daily entertainment plans so you can research them ahead of time.

- Use sites like Yelp and TripAdvisor to research local entertainment and get an idea of the costs ahead of time.
- Consider getting a AAA membership. They offer travel discounts at restaurants and entertainment venues.

3. Consider gifts and souvenirs. Many travelers purchase gifts for others other souvenirs for themselves. It will be difficult to determine the costs ahead of time so make a budget you can stick to.

- Make a list of the people you intend to purchase gifts for ahead of time and try to assign a rough dollar amount.

Part 4

Doing Budget-Friendly Planning

1. Save up some money. Travel can be expensive so developing a comprehensive budget is a great idea.

- You may also need to set aside money from your typical day-to-day expenses so you'll have enough. Work out a regular amount of money to set aside for your travel expenses and begin saving as soon as possible.
- If you need some extra money to make your travel budget, consider a part-time or temporary job like driving for a ride-sharing program or writing for an online publication. Search for temporary jobs on websites like Craigslist, Indeed, or FlexJobs.
- If you're a frequent traveler or have travel benefits from your credit card company, you may be able to defray the costs of airfare or travel.

2. Convert your currency. If you are leaving the country, you may need to exchange your money for the local currency. Use your preferred search engine to find the name of the country you're visiting to determine what type of currency they use. However, many foreign countries that use different currencies also widely accept U.S. Dollars, so you may want to search whether or not this is applicable in your destination.

- Simply enter the amount of money in your travel budget and then change the second box to the currency of your destination country.

3. Consider an all-inclusive vacation. There are a number of agencies that provide all-inclusive vacation packages that can reduce the cost of specific items and make it easier for you to budget. They usually include lodging, food, and entertainment. provisions like tickets to amusement parks or guided tours. Specific packages are usually geared toward couples, singles, and families with children.

- Check out organizations like funjet, Expedia, and Apple Vacations to find package deals.

How to Plan a Honeymoon on a Budget

While many couples share their wedding day with their family and friends, the honeymoon is the time for the new couple to rest, relax, and enjoy one another's company. Weddings often require a substantial financial commitment, though, with the average cost of a wedding in the US reaching $32,000 according to some surveys. A memorable honeymoon doesn't require a big budget, though. By picking local or offseason locations, finding creative accommodations, and being flexible about when and how you get to your destination, you can plan an unforgettable honeymoon without breaking the bank.

Method 1

Picking Affordable Locations

1. Stay domestic. Domestic travel is often more affordable since you do not have to worry about international taxes and fees. Look at destinations within your home nation to save on international flight prices and taxes.

- If you are in the US, for example, you could consider destinations like Hawaii or the Florida Keys for a tropical escape, or cities like New York or Chicago for an urban adventure.
- Look at territories, as well. Flights from major US cities to Puerto Rico, for example, are often affordable because no international taxes are involved.
- If you have airlines rewards miles, cash them in to see where they can get you. Don't sign up for a rewards card, though, just to get miles for your honeymoon, as this can promote debt elsewhere.

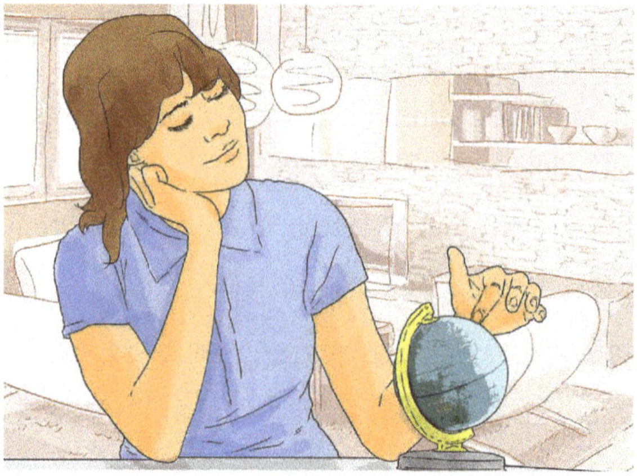

2. Pick a lesser-known destination. Popular destinations such as Jamaica, Costa Rica, and West-

ern Europe are routinely more expensive because of the constant influx of tourist traffic. Research alternative destinations with the features or climate you want to find lower prices.

- Check travel guides online and in print to review activities, climate, and costs of different destinations.
- If you want a honeymoon in a city like Paris with old world charm, for example, look at Canada's Quebec city, which has a wealth of charming French food, architecture, language, and customs for a fraction of the cost.
- If you want a tropical island vacation, instead of planning a trip to sovereign island nations in the Caribbean, look at coastal islands in Brazil and Colombia, which are often much more affordable.

3. Opt for a staycation. Instead of traveling a great distance for your honeymoon, stay nearby and save substantially on the cost of travel. You may choose to get a hotel in the city for a few days, or a cabin out in the country. Just pick a nearby place to unwind and relax after your wedding.

- By eliminating the cost of travel, you can put more of your budget toward accommodations and activities.
- Think about your favorite places and activities in the areas near you. Are there beaches, hiking trails, museums, restaurants, or other activities that you want to share with your new spouse?
- Alternatively, you can opt to find nice, well-appointed accommodations such as a hotel and spa or mountain lodge and spend your time relaxing and unwinding on property.

4. Go camping. Camping is an affordable way to connect with your new spouse and take on an

adventure together. Look at national parks, nature preserves, and areas like forests, lakes, and beaches to find campgrounds that are affordable and easily accessible for you.

- Camping offers you and your spouse the chance to spend some time alone talking and bonding, as well as exploring nature and taking on adventurous activities such as hiking and kayaking together.
- If tents and communal showers aren't your idea of a honeymoon, you can also look at "glamping" properties. These often cost a bit more, but offer more luxury accommodations such as beds, electricity, and private hot-water showers.

Method 2

Finding a Place to Stay

1. Look for vacation rentals. Instead of staying at a resort or hotel, look on sites like Airbnb and FlipKey. These let you find houses, apartments, and other unique property rentals, often for less money than a hotel.

- You can opt to rent anything from a private room to the entire property, and generally get access to amenities such as a kitchen and laundry as well as a bedroom and bathroom.
- These sites also occasionally feature unique rental properties such as tree houses, trailers, remodeled planes, and ships, if you are looking for something to make your trip more memorable.
- When you choose a vacation rental, you can often get recommendations for places to eat and drink as well as things to do from your host. You may even be able to arrange a tour of the area with them.

2. Find an all-inclusive resort. In certain destinations, particularly in Caribbean islands and South Pa-

cific, all-inclusive resorts allow you the chance to pay a single price for everything including your meals, drinks, and certain selected activities. Deals on all-inclusive packages can often be found online.

- Before you book, check online or call the hotel to see what is included with your price. While some properties include only the rooms, meals, and access to the property, others may include activities such as snorkeling and diving as well as spa services.
- All-inclusive resorts generally do not include activities off of the property, so if you are looking to explore around the area, budget that as an additional cost.

3. Check deal sites. Online deal sites such as Groupon often feature deals on hotels and vacation packages. Shop around online to find deals on both your accommodations and activities for your honeymoon.

- Some deal sites offer bargains on full vacation packages that include hotel, flight, and certain tours or planned activities, as well as hotel deals.
- You can also contact hotels directly with prices quoted from deal sites for their hotel or for nearby hotels, and see if you can get them to bargain down from there.

Method 3

Making Logistical Arrangements

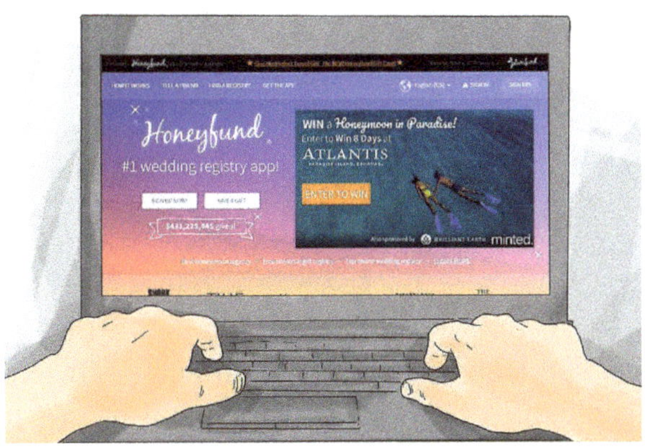

1. Sign up for a honeymoon registry. Instead of registering for home goods, register for your honeymoon. Wedding guests can donate to your honeymoon online, giving amounts for specific activities such as contributing to your flight or buying you dinner for the evening.

- You can register online with sites like Wanderable and Honeyfund.
- Include a link to your registry in your invitations and save-the-date cards, as well as on your wedding webpage.

2. Travel in the off-season. While it's advisable to avoid monsoon and hurricane seasons, many places simply have a high and a low season based on tourist traffic patterns. Look into the low season for your destination and book then to save on flights and hotels.

- Many Caribbean islands, for example, have a high season from December through April due to cold North Americans wanting to escape the winter. Book in the late spring or early fall for better prices.
- Europe, on the other hand, generally experiences the greatest number of tourists in the summer and immediately around Christmas. Book a winter or early spring trip for major savings.

3. Start planning in advance. The sooner you start planning, the better prepared you will be when it comes time to book. Start planning one to two years in advance, if possible, to track flight and hotel prices and find the best time to book.

- Do not wait to book until the last minute. The closer to departure you get, the more the price of flights, trains, hotels, and activities will go up.

4. Find alternative transportation. Look at budget airlines, trains, and busses to get the most affordable ticket to your destination. If you have to fly, look at airports further out from your destination. These often are home to budget carriers which offer cheaper service.

- You may also want to consider driving to your destination. This could offer an affordable alternative to flying or taking a train, and give you and your partner a chance to take a roadtrip together.

5. Plan your meals. Meals are often a large and overlooked expense during a honeymoon. Plan where you are going to eat in advance so that you can set a reasonable budget for going out.

- Treat yourself to one or two truly nice meals, such as a sunset dinner or gourmet breakfast, and opt to dine at more casual restaurants such as cafes and diners the rest of the time.
- You can also cook for yourself if you have an apartment rental, or prepare no-cooking needed meals like salads and sandwiches from your hotel. Pack a romantic picnic for the beach to save money and still make a memory.

6. Wait a while. Save money on your honeymoon by saving money for your honeymoon. Instead of taking it immediately after your wedding, which likely had its own heavy costs associated with it, plan to take your honeymoon at a later time, such as your one year anniversary.

- Create a savings plan such as putting ten percent of each paycheck or $100 a month toward your honeymoon during that period of time.
- Review destinations and costs and start planning in advance during this period to get the best deals.

How to Plan a Family Vacation on a Budget

Money is always an issue in today's world, but that doesn't mean you can't plan a fun vacation on a tight budget, it just takes a few tricks and some smart thinking in order to pull it off. Here are some ideas that should be useful when planning a money-conscious vacation.

Steps

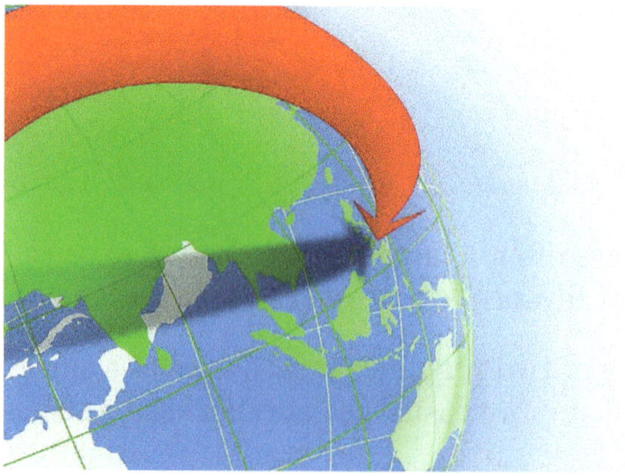

1. Decide how to get there. Assuming that by now you have your destination already picked out, how are you going to get there? Gas prices are near four dollars a gallon, and plane tickets are expensive, not to mention the very strict rules as to what you can and cannot take on board.

- International train travel. Amtrak is the national rail company in the United States. In Europe, consider buying Eurail (for non-EU citizens) or Interrail (for EU citizens) international rail passes.

- International coach travel. In the United States, Greyhound provide bus travel. In Europe, Eurolines provide a pass to cover travel between more than 45 European cities. Megabus provide intercity bus travel in North America and Europe.

- International ship/ferry travel. Cruises can be cheap if you consider accommodation and meals are included. Cunard operate transatlantic cruises. TheCruisePeople compare cruise prices.

- If you Drive. Instead of eating your meals at McDonald's on your way to Vacation, pack a cooler of food. You can buy a cooler and a weeks worth of sandwich stuff for around 25-35 dollars. Get a tune up, they can be expensive but a Tune up will help keep your car fuel efficient and could possibly save your life. Budget at least $20 over what you think you'll be paying in gas.

- If you Fly. Travelocity, or other Internet sites like Expedia can help with finding a cheap rate. Flying at odd hours will ensure a cheaper ticket! When traveling around Europe book your plane for around midnight because those flights offer the lower rates. Whatever airline you book with, look up their site as well and see what their rules are as far as carry on material and flight exchanges or cancellations. You might be able to get a cheaper rate through the airline than through Travelocity, and you can save even more money by bringing food with your carry on, so long as they allow it. In flight snacks are expensive so if you can, pack your own.

2. Where to Sleep

- The best advice on where to stay is to check hotel rooms and rates early, a few months in advance.

- The earlier you book a room the cheaper the rate.

- Also try to book in their off season, many Hotels will have cheaper rates when they don't expect a lot of reservations to be coming in.

3. "I Forgot"

- It's a bummer when you find out that you forgot something important and have to spend money on an item like, a bathing suit, or shampoo. Granted these items can be cheap, but its better not to have to spend money on them.

- Here's what you do to make sure you don't forget anything. Do a walk through of your home and write down all the things you use for personal hygiene, and things you will want to have on your vacation. Tape the list to the top of the suitcase, and the day of your flight... start packing.

- Once you know, that everything on the list is in the suitcase... rip up the list. Its easy and It's a fairly good way to make sure you got everything.

4. Mealtime

- An expensive, but fun pastime during vacation is eating out.

- Plan your meals ahead of time.

- Budget your money and if you can, eat out everyday, if you can afford it.

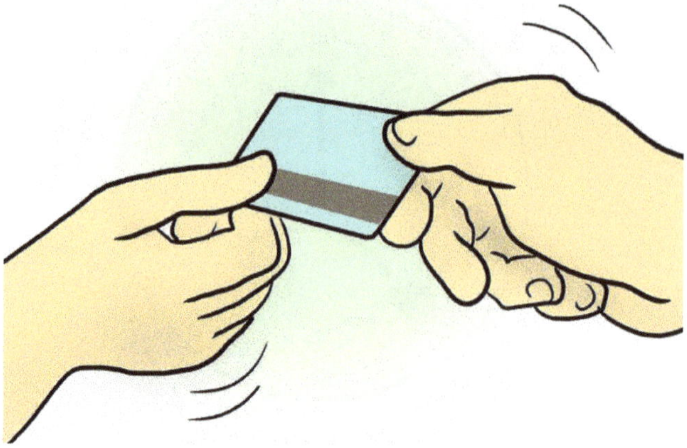

- If you can't, look at your monthly food bill, and estimate how much it will cost for you and your family to eat for the amount of time on the vacation. Then either pack a cooler to take with you, or plan on going shopping at a store near the hotel and fixing picnic-like meals in the room.

- Try to set money aside for at least one meal out at a restaurant, and if you do, make sure it's a place that isn't common to your hometown.

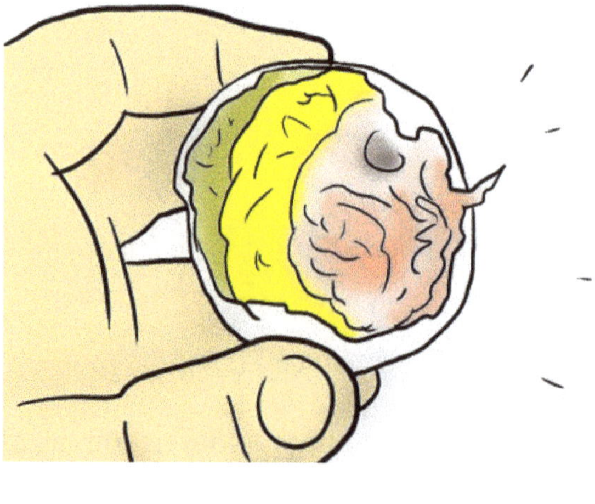

- Make it something different and something fun.

How to Budget Travel for a Single Parent

Single parent households are increasingly common. If you are a single parent working hard to make sure your children have every advantage, then saving for family travel may seem difficult. Travel exposes children to new cultures and teaches them how to adjust to new situations. Single parents can still travel with their families within their country or abroad. It requires saving over a period of months or years, making smart travel purchases and choosing a trip based on what you and your children will enjoy most.

Method 1

Saving for Single Parent Travel

1. Earn miles on a credit card. If you already use and pay off a credit card, then make sure each dollar spent is giving you airline mileage. If you are confident that you can make most of your purchases on a credit card and then pay off the balance each month, you can rack up enough mileage for 1 to 2 plane tickets per year.

- Some airline miles rewards cards give you 2 or more miles for every dollar spent. Make sure you do not choose a card with a dangerously high interest rate, especially if you are uncertain whether you will be able to pay off the balance each month.

- Do not avoid mileage credit cards with an annual fee. Some cards give you 2 miles (3.2 km) per dollar spent, but charge $50 to $100. Doubling your mileage and earning 2 plane tickets will save you money on travel, even if you pay an annual fee.

2. Decide if you would prefer weekend getaways or 1 big trip. Ask your children what they would prefer as well, which will get them more involved with the trip. Several small trips within a day's drive may be more affordable than a week-long trip to another country.

3. Set aside a little bit of money each month. Many banks offer Very Important Purchase (VIP) accounts that let you set up to a certain amount of money aside each month. Although they do not always offer the best interest rates, you can choose how much to put aside and the date when it will become available.

Method 2

Planning Budget Friendly Travel

1. Plan in advance. Last minute travel deals rarely work with kids, because they have plans, camps, school and possible trips to see another parent. Many travel organizations offer discounts to people who book early.

2. Choose your destination based on what your children will enjoy. The best way to curtail complaints and ensure a good time is to define what your children will enjoy most. For example, a child is probably more apt to enjoy a theme park when they are 8 and a European trip when they move into their teenage years.

- Although you may want to go far away for a vacation, you are more likely to believe your hard earned and budgeted money is well spent if your children are excited about the trip.

3. Book a shorter vacation. Children may not crave a 2-week vacation, like many adults do. Short

cruises of 3 to 6 days and packages of 7 days or less will cost less while still affording you time away from home and work.

4. Travel in the off-season. Travel to Europe during the fall and winter. Travel to South America, Central America or the Caribbean in the summer or fall.

- The weather might be rainier and slightly colder or hotter than the peak seasons, but you can save thousands of dollars in airplane tickets, hotels, excursions and other travel costs.

5. Book group travel. There are a few different options for taking advantage of group travel discounts.

- Book a specially organized trip for single parents. Some websites offer exactly this kind of trip. They choose a few destinations each year that include good activities for children. You can choose which trip works best based on your budget.
- Organize a group trip yourself. If you have a sports group, church group or friends with children who are also interested in travel, you can contact a group travel provider and travel agent and ask for quotes on certain destinations. The price will go down as you sign up more people. Ask if travel is free for the group leader.

6. Ask for discounts and specials. Travel agents will try to book your trip without discounts, but they can usually throw something in, if you ask for it. Ask about cruise vouchers, upgrades, free excursions or other incidentals, if they can't offer an up front discount.

- If your children are small and picky eaters, then an all-inclusive package is preferable. Most resorts offer food to please all age levels.

7. Pay a little to the travel company each month. If you book group or all-inclusive travel well in advance, you may be able to pay a few hundred dollars each month, instead of paying a thousand or more dollars all at once. Although you would pay the same amount, you can set up a monthly budget without dipping into your savings.

Method 3

Avoiding Incidental Vacation Spending

1. Book an all-inclusive vacation package. This type of package includes hotels, food and activities.

These are common in Mexico, the Caribbean, Hawaii, in parts of Mediterranean Europe and on cruises.

- Most all-inclusive trips will cost more up front than non-inclusive trips. If you plan to eat and spend time at the resort, you will save money that you would have spent during the vacation.

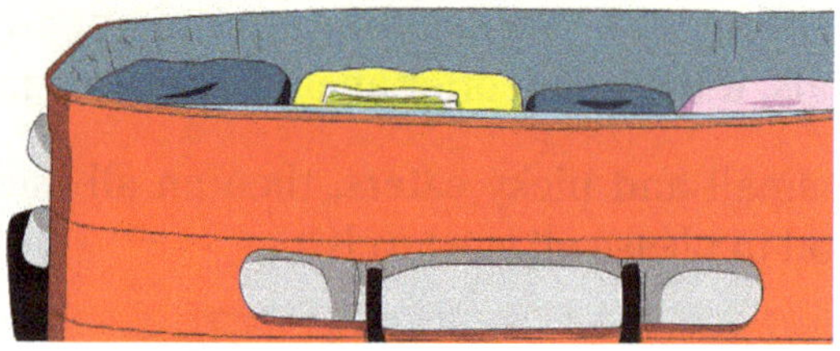

2. Pack minimally. Baggage costs are rising, so try to split a suitcase with your infant or toddler. Baggage weight can also make you less mobile at your destination, so make sure older kids and teenagers pack only what they can wheel or carry in airports and in cities.

- Test your child's baggage before leaving. Ask older kids to cart their suitcase up a flight of stairs and tow it for a mile on city streets. This will help to convince them to pack lightly.

How to Plan a Multi Family Vacation

Getting together has also never been harder given people's increasingly busier lives and the rising cost of nearly every form of travel. Making sure that you make the most of your family get together is important. It all starts with just a little bit of upfront planning.

Steps

1. Put someone in charge of the vacation. When planning a multi-family vacations, put someone in

charge of the vacation. While everyone is responsible for their own itineraries (like plane flights) and special needs, someone is orchestrating the master schedule so that everyone can be on the same page. In this way, decisions can be made quickly, there's a central point of contact for most everything and it reduces confusion and malaise.

2. Decide on the dates, location and the venue and start committing early. Usually everyone has a few places they'd really like to go to. Others have certain places that they absolutely don't want to or can't go to. Everyone has some level of budget restriction. The person in charge of the vacation should solicit all this information from everybody and even delegate some of the research to family members. Early decision making is really important if you want to get your first choice at a reasonable price.

3. Choose the type of housing. Some sample ideas for get together venues are:

- Villa / Vacation Rental – getting one big house with one big kitchen/living room is a great way to spend quality time with the family. There's nothing like being able to stroll into the living room to watch a late night movie with whoever is staying up. Conversations need not be interrupted prematurely and plus there's always a central base that is the hub of activity.
- Cruise – the ultimate in convenience. You don't have to worry about food and you unpack only once. Make sure you get rooms reasonably near each other or else you risk spreading the hub of activity.
- Tours – Some tour companies can customize a tour for your family if you have a minimum

number of people in your group. Many view tours as a the great way to learn more about a place while others may view tours as being too restrictive.

- Hotels / Resorts – suites are a great way to pack more people together and to save on costs by cooking. For large get-togethers though it can be somewhat impersonal because hotel rooms are too small to accommodate everybody for a chat or to play a game and so you end up with dispersed mini-groups within the get together. If you have to book multiple hotel rooms, try to get them all in one wing or even suites that connect if possible. Look for the group discount too -- depending upon the size of your group you may qualify.
- Family member's house – choosing one family member's house to congregate is definitely the cheapest option. You never have to worry about picking the right restaurant and stocking up is easy to do. There are certainly many other wonderful options, like working ranches, Disney World, RV, houseboat, camping, renting that castle in Scotland, taking that trip around America on Amtrak but the key is to get the commitment first. As soon as you agree, start booking. Once people are committed, meaningful planning goes a lot faster and easier.

4. Organize the basics online. You could do this via email, but you will be inundated with a myriad of emails that will add even greater confusion. One source that we have found to be great is to use a group website like PB, where family members can add their own information

- Have everyone put their flights in the group calendar - this makes it easier to coordinate airport pickups and car rental configurations.
- Put local resources and maps in the group site so that everyone will have the latest and greatest information
- Place everyone's cell phone number, pager, instant messenger handles, etc. for quick communication online. Add any other important information such as visa's, shots, temperature and weather patterns and provide that information to all family members.
- Consider booking a few restaurant reservations before your trip. If you have a large group, trying to find a decent restaurant last minute that can accommodate a large party may be impossible.

- Make an online shopping list - have all family members add things that they would like to eat, snack, beach toys etc. Think about setting up a WalMart or Costco run as your first order of business when you get there so you can stock up on the things you need early.

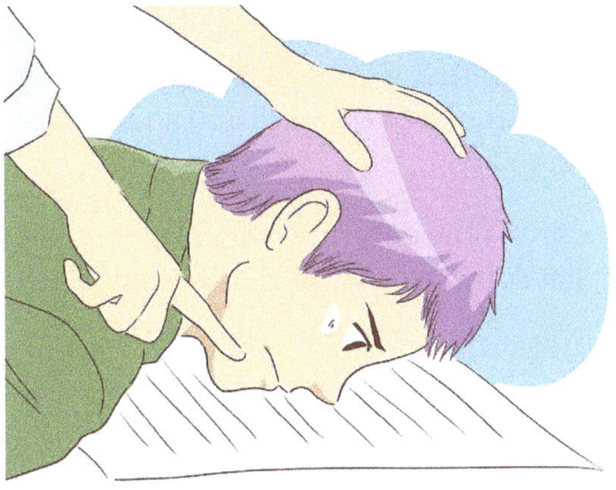

5. Don't be a control freak. Nothing can sap the fun out of a vacation than somebody who can't roll with the punches – and especially for the person who is organizing or helping to organize the vacation. No vacation works out exactly as you plan. Remember that you are having a vacation and that means having fun, not making sure everything on the planned itinerary is checked off. Also I usually only plan at most 2 things in a day. Getting so many people coordinated is difficult already and any transitions between activities takes more time than you think. Somebody always wants to visit that gift shop for a little bit extra time or to take that side diversion and you have to be able to accommodate for that.

6. But do plan activities. The purpose of a family vacation is to have family spend time with each other and especially to engage with each other in conversation. A couple of ideas to make sure you include everybody and increase those memorable moments...

- Cooking meals together – it's certainly cheaper to eat inside but the bigger benefit is that you get people working together in the kitchen talking. And there's nothing like being able to share your food repertoire with your family members. (have an online sign-up sheet where families can sign-up for dinner duty)
- Slide show – family slide shows are only boring to those who aren't in the family. Seeing baby pictures, embarrassing photos and swapping stories are a great way to get the family

laughing together. PowerPoint and a projector are the best way but bringing a DVD with all of the goods is another great way to get some great laughs.

- Video Games? -- well it depends. For most families, banning video games are essential to prevent the children from spending their entire vacation in front of the television. However there are many group participation games that are a blast for groups. On the Wii for instance, there's Rock Band, Karaoke type games and a multitude of brain teaser and puzzler games that are fun for everybody.
- Exercise – the Kennedy's aren't the only ones who play football when they get together. Get people out on the court, get some exercise and have some fun.

7. Deal with the money early. It's good to work out a system with regards to shared costs early so there is no misunderstanding. Some families prefer to spend everything separate by family while others pay up front and say "pay me later." For the latter, it's important to work out a good way to distribute the costs fairly. Some families keep track of every dish that is ordered and while that is clearly the fairest way, it's also requires the most effort. In my last vacation we had 4 families. For shared costs like meals, we split it up by number of adults and number of kids (we counted each kid as half an adult) so that we could simplify the calculation. It's never perfect, but why worry about nickel and dime among family. Everyone should keep their receipts and ideally, you spend the last day putting stuff into a spreadsheet so that you can settle up that day or at least soon after the vacation.

8. Start talking about the next vacation – you can't beat face-to-face communication. Spend a little time on the last day talking about what you want to do for the next vacation. You can get a lot done

talking about it in person in a group versus over email or over the phone and plus you'll be fresh with the knowledge of what worked well and what didn't.

9. Keep the vacation spirit alive. - make sure everyone gets back fine by sending an email or making a phone call. Do some photo sharing and if you are enterprising, put together a photo book so that you can always remember the good times.

How to Plan Activities for Solo Travel

Many people are nervous about travelling alone and are worried about feeling lonely. That does not have to be the case. There are a number of benefits to solo travel and it can actually be a very rewarding experience. You don't have to worry about waiting on other people or negotiating activities. Instead, you can spend your time and money engaging in things that interest you. In order to plan activities for solo travel, you should focus on your own interests, find ways to meet new people, and take extra safety precautions.

Method 1

Focusing on your Interests

1. Prioritize your budget to reflect what you enjoy. Traveling alone can be pricey because you are

unable to share costs with a partner or friend. For example, accommodations are often more expensive for an individual traveller. Despite this drawback, you will be able to spend money engaging in activities that interest you. When traveling with others, you often have negotiate and accommodate the interests of others.

- As a solo traveler you can choose to spend money on the activities that really interest you.
- For example, you might want to splurge on an expensive meal or spend money taking in a local show.

2. Plan activities that interest you. Maybe you have always wanted to hike Kilimanjaro, but none of your friends or family are fit enough. Alternatively, you may be interested in visiting obscure historical sites and museums that do not appeal to your usual travel companions. Take advantage of your time as a solo traveler and engage in activities that only appeal to you.

- Research all of the sites that your destination has to offer and spend your time experiencing the ones that interest you the most.

3. Embrace your alone time. Keep in mind that there is a reason you decided to embark on a solo trip. Although it is fun to meet new people and find travel buddies, you should not be afraid to embrace some alone time. Walk through the city alone and take in the sights and sounds. Allow yourself to get lost in your thoughts as you sit on a beach watching the waves.

Method 2

Avoiding Isolation While Traveling Alone

1. Sign up for group trips and tours. If you want to travel solo but don't want to feel completely alone, you can sign up for group trips and tours. These can often be a great way to safely travel by yourself and you will meet a lot of new people to share in your travel experiences. If an entire group trip does not appeal to you, combine some group-based activities with solo time.

- For example, you could take a five day bus tour through Italy and then spend three days exploring Rome on your own.
- Research and book group trips ahead of time.
- Typically, the more expensive the tour, the older the demographic.

2. Stay in hostels or B&Bs. If you are worried about feeling lonely while traveling, do not isolate yourself in a 5-star hotel. Although glamorous, large hotels are not the best places to meet people. Instead, you should stay in a more community-oriented space, such as a hostel or bed and breakfast.

- At a hostel it is easy to meet fellow travelers and many will have group tours offered through the hostel. You can opt to pay a bit more for a single room, if you are not interested in sharing your sleeping space with strangers.

- B&B's are a great place to meet locals who can give you amazing dining and travel tips. The owners are usually very eager to share information about the local culture and B&Bs often feel more homey than a large hotel.

3. Talk to strangers. Don't be afraid to meet people and talk to strangers. While you are traveling on your own, you will find that it is actually quite easy to meet people. Strike up a conversation with anyone who looks friendly. One way to meet people is by offering to take someone's picture. Then you can begin a conversation from there.

- Alternatively, you could head to a local bar and strike up a conversation with the bartender or other patrons. You could say something like "I hear California Sushi has the best sushi in town. Is that true?" Locals will be eager to give you their opinion.
- Another way to meet people when you are traveling in a large city, is to ask people where they are from. Most people, even those living in the city, have likely migrated there for work. This can often lead to fun and interesting conversations.

4. Use social media to connect with people. There are a growing number of social media-based apps that can connect travelers. These can be a great way to easily meet like-minded individuals while traveling. Try out some of these sites:

- Meetup is a site where you can meet up with a group of people for a variety of different events including photography walks, happy hour, picnics etc.
- Leaplocal will connect you with local guides who can show you around.

- Couchsurfing is a way to find accommodations by staying with a local. This is a great way to meet new people.

5. Stay in touch with family and friends at home. You can also fight the feelings of isolation by keeping in touch with your family and friends back home. For example, schedule a Skype call periodically throughout your trip. You can also post pictures from your trip onto social media sites, such as Facebook or Instagram. This will allow your friends and family to comment and engage with you, while you are traveling.

- Keeping in touch is also a good safety precaution. This allows your friends and family to know where you are throughout your trip.

Method 3

Dining as a Solo Traveler

1. Sit at the bar. Dining alone can feel uncomfortable, but it doesn't have to. Try sitting at a lunch counter or bar. This way you will be seated next to strangers and you can easily try and strike up a conversation. You can also talk with the bartender or other servers as they are working. This is a great way to meet people and sit in a restaurant without feeling lonely.

2. Have things to do while you eat. Another thing you can do while dining alone is bring something to occupy your mind. For example, if you are out for lunch or breakfast you could try reading a newspaper or doing a crossword while you eat.

- Alternatively, you could bring a notebook to dinner with you. Write down notes about your day or some of the food you are eating.
- You could also try reading a novel while you wait for your meal to arrive.

3. Eat with locals. If you go to a restaurant during a busy time as a solo traveler, you may get seated with other singles or at a larger group table. This is a great way to meet local people and engage in conversation while dining. You could also try frequenting the same restaurant. This way the staff will get to know you and you will become comfortable chatting with them.

Method 4

Staying Safe While Traveling Alone

1. Trust your instincts. The best way to stay safe while traveling alone is by trusting your instincts.

If you find yourself in a situation and you feel uncomfortable, you should try to remove yourself immediately from that environment. For example, maybe you find the hostel owner overly pushy or intrusive. Trust your instincts and find other accommodations. Although you may have to spend a bit more money, it is better to be safe.

2. Be aware of your surroundings. When traveling by yourself, you do not have a friend to look out for you. As a result, you will need to pay particular attention to your surroundings at all times. Keep your belongings close to you while traveling and never leave them unattended. Avoid looking at your phone while traveling through public spaces. Instead, you should look up periodically to assess your surroundings.

3. Keep money and important documentation safe. Do not carry all of your money around with you. Instead, you should separate your cash into different bags. That way if something gets stolen, you will not lose all of your money at once. You should also always carry your passport with you, or place it in a locked safe.

- Take photocopies of your passport and any other important travel documents. That way you will have a backup copy available if anything should happen.

CHAPTER 3 Ticket Booking Techniques

Travel agents book tickets that would enable customers to travel to the venue or region of their choice. Sticking to a budget should be an important concern for the travel agent. Emergencies such as cancellation of flights, changes in schedule, etc. are situations that a travel agent must be prepared for. The aspects elucidated in this chapter are of vital importance, and provide a better understanding of ticket booking.

How to Check Flight Reservations

Whether you book your airline tickets online, by phone, or through a travel agent, it is always a good idea to check your reservations before the day of departure. When you check your flights, you can choose your seats, purchase meals, and make requests for any special accommodations you might need. Try to verify your flight information beforehand, make any special requests, and be prepared to check-in the day of travel.

Method 1

Confirming Flight details and Information

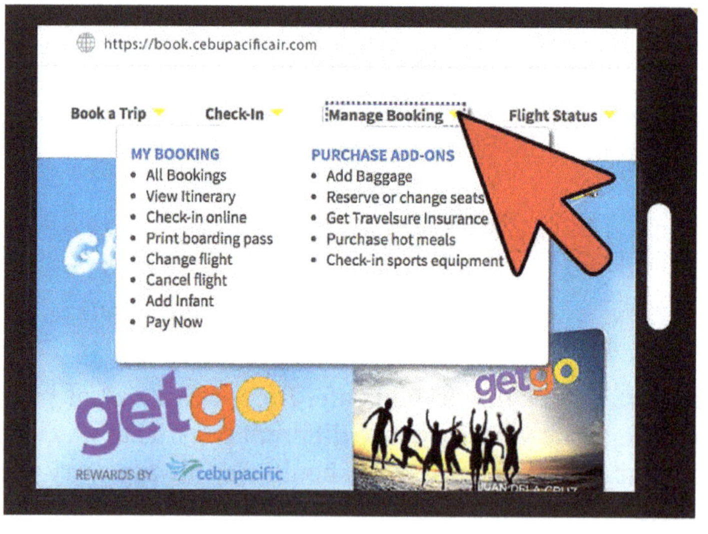

1. Visit the airline website to check in and confirm details. Navigate online to the airline website, or click the "Register" button on the confirmation email that the airline sent you when you booked your flight. Once you navigate the check-in menus, you should see your flight information, including the number of travelers, departure and arrival times and cities.

- Even if you initially booked your flight through a travel company (such as Expedia or Priceline), you should still register for your flight through the airline website. You may be able to confirm flight details through the travel company website, but you'll need to check in to the flight and purchase special requests through the airline site.

2. Check your boarding information. At this point, you can also view your boarding pass, and find out your seat assignment and boarding zone. If you do not have your reservation number, you might be able to find your boarding information using your flight number and your last name. Check the e-mail you received when you purchased the ticket to find your reservation or ticket number.

3. Confirm your reservation details. When checking in prior to a flight, it's always good to check to make sure the specific details of your flight have not changed. Visit the airline's webpage and, using the flight Confirmation Number you've been sent, check online to make sure that you have the correct flight number and destination.

- You can also check on specific details of your original reservation to confirm the date, location, and time of your flight. To do this, click on the web-page tab that says "Manage Reservation," "My Trips," or "My Trips/Check-In." Each airline will have a different name for this tab, but it should be easy to locate.

4. Check your flight's departure time. When you're checking in online, look to see if your flight has been delayed or canceled. This information should be easily accessible: look in the email that the airline sent you when you reserved your flight, and check the flight time. Then, enter the Confirmation Number on the airline's website, and check that the departure and arrival times have not changed.

- If your flight has been substantially delayed, the airline will likely inform you through email or a text message.

Method 2

Checking on Special Requests Online

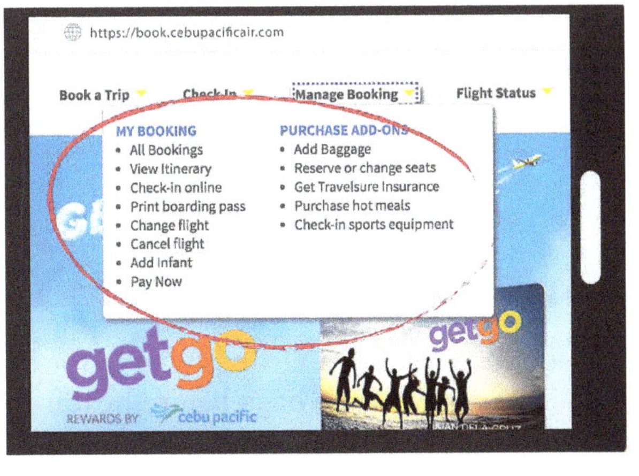

1. Note special requests on the airline website while checking in. Once you've checked your reservation, you can check the airline's options for ordering meals, checking in pets, checking luggage and choosing your seats. After you have finished checking or making changes to your reservation, you can verify the reservation online.

- Know that changing any flight information after making your reservation may cost extra. If possible, try to make sure all your special requests are in by the time you make the reservation.

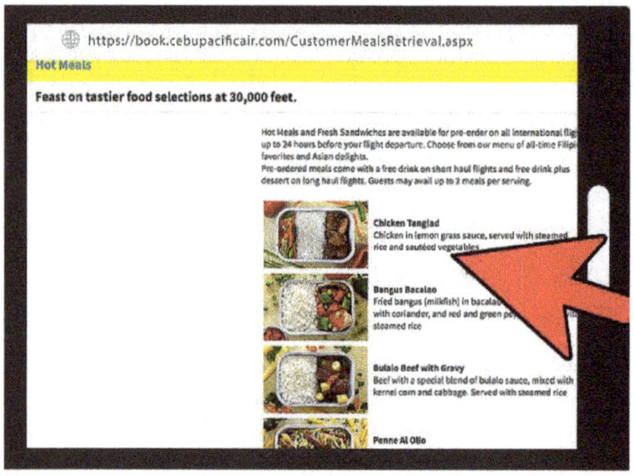

2. Order meals to eat during the flight. While confirming your flight, you may have the option to choose meals for your flight. Be prepared to pay for them, since most domestic flights no longer include free meals. Each airline has slightly different food policies and options, so make sure you know what is available on your carrier.

- Contact the airline in advance if you have any unique dietary restrictions or food allergies. Call the airline directly or contact them via e-mail if you need special food or have severe food allergies so they will be prepared the day of the flight. There should be a number of options that are available for a variety of diets.
- International flights often offer complimentary meals.

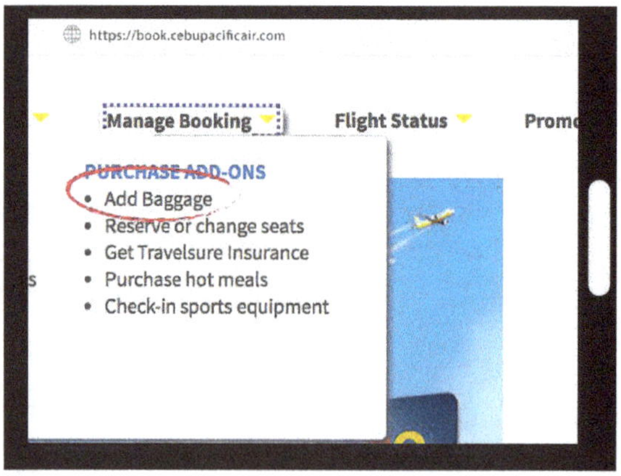

3. Pay for checked and carry-on luggage. Most airlines charge for both checked and carry-on luggage. Make sure to check-in and pay for all bags before heading to the airport. If you did not pay for checked or carry-on bags when making the initial flight reservation, you can pay for bags when checking in online for your flight, or at your airline's service desk in the airport terminal.

- If you know how many bags you will be checking, enter the number and pay for them ahead of departure with a credit card.

- Checked and carry-on luggage is often more expensive in the 24 hours leading up to the flight than prior to that time period. Plan to pay all baggage fees well in advance.

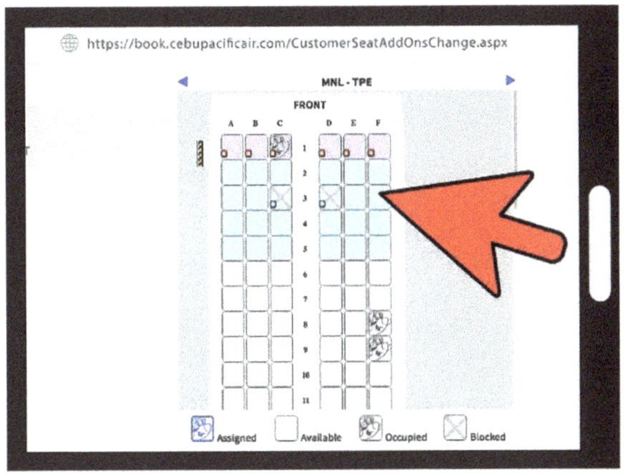

4. Choose seats on your flights. For most airlines, you can specify the seat type you prefer (window or aisle) or choose your specific seat, if a seat hasn't already been assigned to you. Some airlines have individual fees for different types of seats, while others charge more for first-class seating or seats with extra leg room.

- Most airlines will allow you to choose your seats ahead of time. Check in and find the seat that's in the best location for your travel.

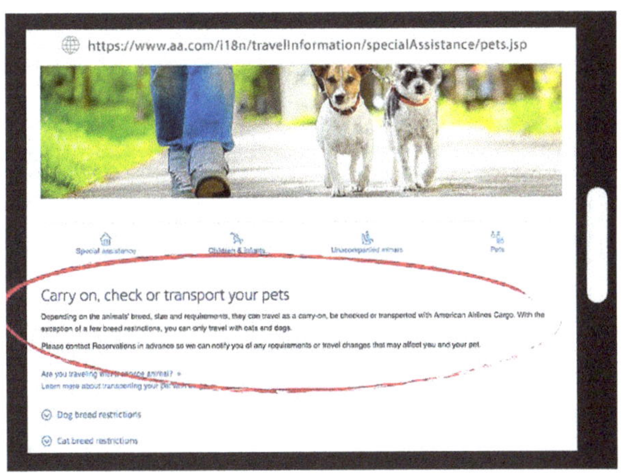

5. Check in pets. If you are traveling with pets, make sure you've verified all details with the airlines beforehand. Flying with pets can be logistically difficult, and you'll want to know that everything is ready when you arrive for your flight. Smaller pets can sometimes be taken as carry-ons. Verify your kennel meets the appropriate sizes and regulation for the airline. Larger animals cannot be carried on and need to be kept underneath the cabin.

- There are size requirements for both carry-on kennels and checked kennels. You can find these guidelines on your airline's website or by calling the airline's "Contact Us" number.
- Make sure that you check in advance about any special weather restrictions. Airlines often have travel restrictions for pets based on the time of the year. Verify with your airline that you will meet the appropriate restrictions during the time of your flight.

Method 3

Checking In the Day of your Flight

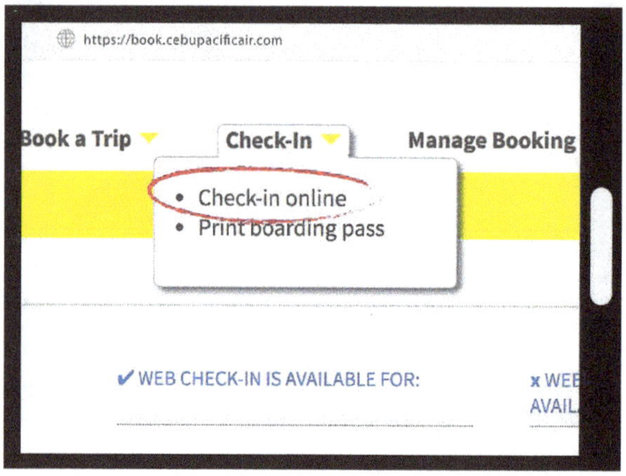

1. Check in 24 hours in advance. You can do this by navigating to the website of your airline, and find the section of the website where you can "Check In". Once you've verified all of your flight information, you're ready to do the final check-in. Input your reservation number or flight number. You may need other additional information to confirm your identity.

- Make sure to check-in all final baggage, seats, and pets online prior to your flight time.
- Finalize all baggage, seats, and pets on your check-in. If you added them beforehand, verify that these special requests are all being honored by the airline.

2. Check in at the airport terminal. After you've checked your online check-in, you'll be ready to complete the final check-in at the airport. Bring your driver's license, passport, or other government-issued photo ID when you travel, as the airline will need to verify your identity. Airport terminals are busy places, so being ready to show the attendant all necessary documents will make sure you get through the line quickly and easily.

- Print your flight confirmation or boarding pass at the terminal kiosk when you arrive at the airport. If you think you'll be in a rush once you arrive at the airport, you can also print your boarding pass once you have checked in to your flight online.

3. Bring checked luggage to the drop-off location. Make sure you have your checked luggage ready to give to the attendant at the terminal. Keep your luggage secure and ready to be kept under the plane. Before checking your luggage, verify that your checked luggage meets the weight requirements. Most airlines charge extra for luggage over 50 pounds.

- Keep your luggage well marked and easy to locate. Much luggage looks the same. Do something to make your luggage distinctive so you'll recognize it when you see it again at your arrival destination.

4. Bring your checked pets to the airline desk. If you're traveling with pets, make sure your pets are secure and ready to travel in their kennel. They need to have been fed and be calm for the flight. Give yourself extra time to check your pets, so the attendant can verify your paperwork.

- Pets usually need to be a minimum age to fly. Most airlines suggest 6 to 8 weeks.
- Small dogs and cats also need to have a health certificate issued by a vet close to the time of departure and arrival. How recent the health certificate needs to be depends on the airline.

5. Prepare your carry-on luggage. Small bags can be carried onto the plane. However, it is important that both meet the requirements for carry-on luggage and are easy to store in the cabin. Make sure your carry-on bag meets the size requirements. Most carry-on bags need to be able to fit into the overhead compartment. Airports usually have a measurement box so you can test out your baggage.

- Verify that your baggage is not too heavy. Heavy baggage can make it difficult to maneuver around the plane and in the terminal.

6. Prepare pets for the plane. Small pets can also be carried on the plane, although they may need to be kept in a kennel under the seat in front of you. Verify also that your pet is calm and ready to fly. You don't want to have a noisy pet when you come onto the airplane. Noisy pets make for a long and annoying plane ride for your fellow passengers.

- Before boarding, make sure your pet kennel meets the required size and weight requirements. You can find the size and weight requirements on your airline's website.

How to Buy Cheap Airline Tickets

With an influx of studies about the best time to buy airline tickets, search engines that aggregate the prices of dozens of travel websites, and airlines accommodating the strained wallets of most people post-2008 economic downturn, booking cheap airline tickets is easier than ever. Keep reading for detailed information on how to take advantage of all of the tools at your disposal to ensure that you get the best deal on your vacation. To get as much bang for your buck, you'll have to start planning months in advance and secure refunds if a ticket price dips below what you paid for. It is always advisable to shortlist two to three destinations and work towards the one which offers savings in all aspects.

Steps

1. Plan in advance and sign up for email alerts about low-fare deals. To ensure you get the best deals, you should know at least 3 months in advance that you want to take a trip somewhere. If you have a specific destination in mind, sign up for a low-fare alert from Yapta or AirfareWatchdog. Make sure you include nearby departure and arrival airports when you sign up -- you might get more emails, but it'll be well-worth the savings in cost.

- If you don't have a specific destination in mind, sign up for email alerts about the cheapest tickets from a particular departure airport (and any nearby airports). AirfareWatchdog also organizes the best prices for flights from a particular city and to a particular city, so you can prepare the most cost-effective, multi-destination itinerary.
- AirfareWatchdog has real people, not computers, vet deals they hear about to ensure that the sales to which they alert customers are *actually* worthwhile.

2. Know the best time in advance to book tickets. According to studies cited by The New York

Times, international flights have been the cheapest 3-5 months in advance, but there is variation among different regions. Domestic flights are a bit trickier to pin-point, but it's a good idea to start searching 3-4 months in advance and see if they get any cheaper week after week -- there have been studies indicating a 6-weeks-in-advance sweet spot for domestic flight booking.

3. Know when airfare prices are typically the lowest. Airlines generally release sales for specific routes Monday night because they want travel agencies to catch wind of sales early in the week. Deals are then matched by competitors Tuesday morning. Therefore, your best shot at these deals is by searching for flights Tuesday and Wednesday afternoon or evening.

- Keep in mind that fares will be highest on the weekend. Airlines know that's the most convenient time for people to think about vacation plans, so they markup their prices then. Sales released early in the week are also gone by the weekend. Moreover, airlines don't manage their inventory as much on the weekend because they have fewer staffers on hand -- so if a few tickets sell for a specific route, prices will automatically jump higher because computer algorithms perceive an increased demand.
- It's a good idea to do a cursory search for specific routes of interest on several days of the week (including weekends) at least a before you are planning to book, so you have an idea of how much the tickets cost. That way, you can identify a sale when it appears.

4. Use aggregator sites to search for fares. There are simply too many different airline and travel websites for you to make individual queries in each one, so use search engine Software. It not only aggregates dozens of airline and travel websites to give you the best price, but it also has a low-fare calendar so you can see which are the cheapest days to travel in a 30-day period. You can also easily include nearby airports in your search.

- Not every airline/travel website is included in ITA Software, so you may want to visit favorite airlines separately. Also, if you know that a certain airline operates out of a particular destination or specializes in certain routes (e.g., Southwest for flights in the western U.S., Hawaiian Air for flights in the Asia-Pacific, etc.), you may want to make those searches separately to make sure you're not missing the best deals.
- AirfareWatchdog allows you to make searches at individual sites with just a few clicks. Search for a flight, and a box will pop up asking you which sites you'd like to visit. Each logo or link you click on will open the search in a new window.
- According to FareCompare, the cheapest day to fly is Wednesday, followed by Tuesday and Saturday. Friday and Sunday are the most expensive -- naturally, as many seek weekend getaways. But this can vary among destinations and months, so use a low-fare calendar to be sure you're getting the best price.

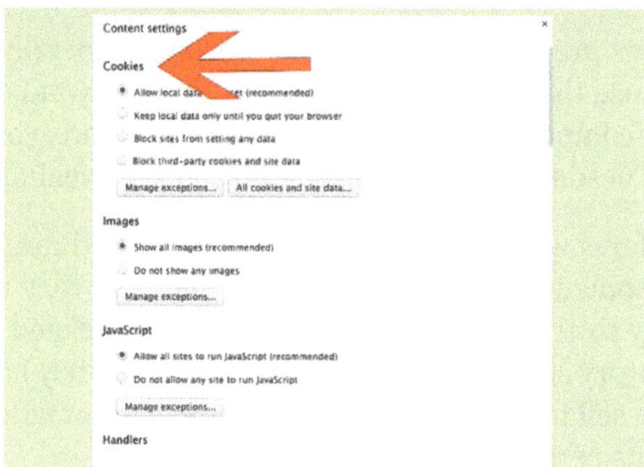

5. Clear out your cache and cookies in between airline searches, especially on different days or weeks. Otherwise, old prices will sometimes display in lieu of new ones, and you may miss out on the best price.

6. For advanced airfare sleuths, consider piecing together flights by hand with cost-saving characteristics. Here are several methods to consider:

- Instead of searching for round-trip tickets, search for two one-way tickets separately. Sometimes purchasing separate tickets on unaffiliated carriers will save you money.

- Search for red-eye flights and other unpopular times. Because of supply and demand, it is going to be more expensive to fly during a convenient time like 10 a.m. than in the middle of the night at 11 p.m.
- Shop as though you are from another country if flying from one international location to another international location. You may save even more by not purchasing in your home country. For example, let's say you are an American and you want to fly from Thailand to Vancouver, Canada. Your best bet to search for prices in Thailand, not the US, as this fare is best priced from that market. US booking engines typically give a higher price.
- If traveling around the holidays, know it is generally cheaper to fly on the holiday itself. People generally want to relax on holidays, and not deal with the hassles of air travel, so tickets are sometimes cheaper then.

7. Consider purchasing through consolidators, which buy bulk tickets in advance to select routes with certain carriers.

- To find a consolidator that works best for you, research the Sunday travel sections of newspapers in big U.S. cities that have a huge population of the country you want to visit. For example, if you want to travel to Israel, New York Sunday newspapers will probably be your best bet. The Israeli population is big in NY and you will find plenty of consolidators advertising to this community for travel to Israel.
- Note that buying through a consolidator may make it difficult or impossible for you to change plans once you have booked your ticket.

8. After you purchase your ticket, don't unsubscribe from those email alerts! Continue watching those prices just in case they drop significantly below what you paid. If that happens, use Yapta to help you get a refund from your airline.

9. Airlines keep coming up with promotional fares for their low selling flights.So In case the destination for which the low fare is offered suits you, the airline can send you an email alert during the promotion.It is also advisable to sign up with the airline websites as well.

How to Buy a Last Minute Cheap Flight

Finding last minute cheap flights will vary upon your travel destination and the time of year you wish to travel. There are, however, many ways to find the cheapest last minute flights for your destination. As well as an abundance of websites that specialize in last minute bookings, there are travel agents, newspapers and special flights that you can find to get the best deals. Generally, you will receive the best deals on flights by booking early, but if you are flexible and need to book at the last minute, you can still save money on airfares. Here are a few steps on how to buy a last minute cheap flight.

Steps

1. Check airline newsletters, websites that specialize in last minute air travel and the travel section of your local newspaper to find last minute deals on flights. Sometimes you can save money by booking flights late because airlines that have not filled their planes will offer discount fares.

2. Compare airfares from different airlines, websites and travel agencies. Purchasing flights directly from the airline is not always the cheapest deal, so check out a few different travel websites and travel agencies to compare prices.

3. Search for flights during undesirable days and times. Fridays, Saturdays and Mondays are usually the busiest flight days for people to travel, so consider booking flights for Tuesdays or Wednesdays, the quietest days for travel. If you are flying around a national holiday, consider flying on the holiday, when most people are already at their destination, rather than the day before.

4. Use your special status if you have any to find discount flights. Some websites offer discount travel to students, teachers, military personnel and the elderly. If you fit into any of these categories, it may be beneficial to book through a company that offers discounts on flights.

5. Consider flying with a discount airline. There are many discount airlines both within the United States and outside of the United States. Discount airlines typically offer discount airfares but sometimes charge extra fees for checked baggage, food and drinks. If you are comfortable without some of these flying luxuries, you may be able to find cheap airfares for last minute flights.

6. Bid on airfares to try to get cheap last minute flights. There are a few websites where you can place a bid on airfares by stating the date you wish to travel and the destination. Once your bid is accepted you will be shown the time of the flight and the airline. Keep in mind that bidding on a flight requires some flexibility in your schedule.

7. Use the frequent flyer miles that you have acquired to purchase a flight at the last minute. You do not generally need to have enough miles to purchase an entire flight, but sometimes you can use acquired frequent flyer miles to reduce the price of a flight you want to purchase.

How to Buy Bulk Airline Tickets

Whether you frequently travel for business or pleasure, or you're in charge of coordinating air travel for a large group trip, buying tickets in bulk can help you save money and stress. Booking directly through a consolidator or an airline can help you access excellent deals for yourself or your group. Using a travel agent's expertise can help you book the best deal on your flights and reduce your stress when coordinating large group travel.

Method 1

Nailing down your Travel Requirements

1. Determine your destinations. Before you can book bulk tickets, you need to know which cities you will be traveling between. This might be the same two cities on a regular basis if you travel for business, or it might be multiple cities at different times if you're booking a one-time trip for a large group.

- For example, if you travel for business you might need 10 flights between Boston and St. Louis to cover your air travel for 3 months.
- If you're planning a large group trip, you might need a flight between JFK airport, Paris, London, and back to JFK for 30 people.
- Consider this information carefully and have it easily accessible when you're ready to book.

2. Determine how many people are going. If you're booking business travel for yourself, you know you only need to arrange air travel for one. If you're booking for a large group, you need to have a final number of travelers before you book.

- If you're booking group travel, you'll need to know this final number a considerable amount of time before you plan to travel, usually several months.

3. Work out your travel time frame. You'll need to know what the time frame is for your travel. If you're booking business travel, you'll probably have a regular travel schedule, with set dates each week (or every few weeks). If you're booking for a group, this might be slightly more flexible, but you'll need to know roughly how long you plan to spend in each location.

- For example, if you're traveling for business, you might know that you leave Boston every second Tuesday for St. Louis, and that you'll return from St. Louis the following Friday.
- If you're booking group travel, you might know that you're leaving JFK for Paris in late May, spending approximately 10 days in Paris before leaving for London, and then spending four days in London before returning to JFK.
- If you have any flexibility in your travel dates, you should have this information easily accessible when you're ready to book.

4. Collect traveler information before you book. Before you can book air travel for other travelers, make sure you have everyone's information. This includes full legal names, addresses, and birthdays.

- Double check the spelling of names if you are booking for others – the names on their tickets must match the names exactly on the IDs they use (driver's license or passport, etc) for them to be able to travel.

Method 2

Booking Through a Consolidator

1. Find a consolidator. Consolidators are companies that buy bulk plane tickets at wholesale prices directly from airlines, and then sell them at greatly reduced rates to others. Using a consolidator will likely get you a better rate than you could on your own through an airline or travel website.

- Some examples of consolidators are: 1-800-FlyEurope, Airfare, AirfarePlanet, Airline-Consolidator, AirTreks, BargainTravel, CheapTickets, Economytravel, Globester, and TFI Tours.
- You can also look for consolidators in the travel section of most major Sunday newspapers.
- Consolidators are different than discount airlines – they do not actually own planes, they just have access to deeply discounted tickets.
- Some travel websites, like Travelocity and Expedia, sometimes offer consolidator fares on certain flights, but they are not actually consolidators. Generally, such websites only offer published fares. Consolidators, on the other hand, offer fares that are not published, and are worked out between the consolidator and the airline.

2. Check their reputation. Consolidators pop up and fold quite frequently, so you need to check the reputation of the consolidator that you use. Check to see if they belong to a consolidator trade organization.

- Look for membership in organizations like the United States Air Consolidators Association (USACA), American Society of Travel Agents (ASTA), or the United States Tour Operators Association (USTOA).
- You should also check to see if anyone has reported the consolidator you've chosen to the Better Business Bureau (BBB). The consolidator should have good BBB reports and scores.

3. Check restrictions on bookings. When using a consolidator, check what restrictions there are on tickets you purchase through them. When you book with a consolidator, you usually can't use frequent flyer miles to pay for your ticket. Additionally, the tickets are probably nontransferable and nonrefundable.

4. Don't be afraid to ask questions. Make sure you ask plenty of questions while you're purchasing your tickets. Different consolidators have different policies, so you want to make sure you get all the details specific to your consolidator. You can either do this by calling the consolidator's customer service phone number and booking over the phone or using the website's chat box, although calling customer service will probably be faster.

- For example, find out if the consolidator has an emergency number to call in case of problems with your travel. Ask what happens if you miss your flights – the original flight or any connections. You should also ask if there are any fees associated with purchasing through them, on top of the price of the ticket.

5. Use a major credit card to book. If you can, use a major credit card to book your travel through a consolidator. This can be a personal or business credit card. Using a major credit card gives you recourse if you don't get a valid ticket because you can deny payment to the consolidator through your credit card company.

6. Confirm your reservation with the airline. Before you pay for your ticket through the consolidator, contact the airline and make sure they have your reservation in process. This way you know the consolidator is doing what they're supposed to be doing on their end. You should also check with the airline again after you pay.

7. Get a record locator number from the consolidator. Once you've booked your travel with the

consolidator, ask for a record locator number (this might also be a confirmation number). This gives you proof that you booked your tickets through the consolidator and gives you a reference number in case you need to contact the consolidator later.

Method 3

Booking Through an Airline

1. Purchase a commuter book. Some airlines offer what's called a commuter book (or, alternatively, airpass memberships). Commuter books are books of coupons (usually 10) that can each be redeemed for one one-way flight between two specific airports on that airline. You pay one set amount for the book and can then use the coupons to book flights any time in the future. These are an especially good option if you know you'll need to be traveling frequently between the same places but aren't sure of exact dates yet.

- The price of the commuter books varies depending on where you're flying from and to, so it's best to shop around before you choose one. If you usually fly in one area of the country, look for commuter books through regional, rather than national, airlines.
- Once you're ready to book your flight, you'll input your traveler information and seat preference like you would when making any other flight reservation, but instead of putting in credit card information to pay, you'll enter the code off of one of the coupons in your book. Keep in mind that you may have to pay extra for things like flight insurance.

2. Look for flat rate tickets. Some airlines provide flat rate tickets for a limited time. Purchasing a flat rate ticket allows you to buy one ticket that you can use as frequently as you want within a

certain time frame. These tickets are more expensive than a regular one-way or round-trip ticket, but it can work out to be much cheaper than booking multiple individual round trips.

- Make sure you double check the details of any flat rate tickets you're interested in purchasing: you might be restricted in the airports you can use or the cities you can fly to.
- With a flat rate ticket, the booking process works the same way as any other booking, but you would enter the information from your flat rate ticket instead of your credit card information.
- There are now third-party apps and subscription services, like OneGo, that allow you to purchase a flight subscription for a set amount per month and give you the freedom to book with more than one airline. These are a great option for very frequent business travelers.

3. Call the airline group reservation desk directly. If you're booking large group travel, call the airline's group reservation desk directly. Their representatives have considerable experience booking air travel for large groups, and they can help guide you through it.

- Before you decide on one airline, call a few different group reservation desks to compare prices as well as flight details. It might work out that you can get a better rate or better flights if you book the different legs of your flights on different airlines.
- When you're ready to book a group flight directly through an airline, make sure you have all of the travelers' information in front of you: their full legal names, the type of ID they'll be using, their addresses, and their birthdates. The airline's group reservation agent will need this information to reserve your block of seats and issue boarding passes for all of the members of your group.

4. Reserve your flight at the right time. If you're booking for a group, you want to reserve your

flights approximately 8 to 10 months before your planned departure. Airlines release individual seats for specific flights up to a year in advance, but they don't release groups seats until later.

- Airlines release group seats at slightly different times, so check the specific timeframe for group seats with your airline.

Method 4

Booking Through a Travel Agent

1. Check their credentials. As with a consolidator, make sure that the travel agent you use is a member of a professional organization, like the Universal Federation of Travel Agents Association (UFTAA) or National Association of Career Travel Agents (NACTA). You can also look up reviews of travel agents on the Consumer Affairs website or the Better Business Bureau.

2. Meet your travel agent in person. Whether you're booking business flight for yourself or group travel for others, it's best to meet with your travel agent for the first time in person. This gives you the chance to meet the agent, discuss your specific travel needs, and have a longer conversation than the phone or email allow.

3. Ask questions. Make sure you ask your travel agents plenty of questions to clarify the details of your trip. You should know if there are there fees on top of the price of the ticket and if there is a help hotline you can call if your travel plans are disrupted.

- You should also ask your travel agent the best way to communicate with them – do they prefer the phone or email? This is particularly important if you need to contact them while you travel.

4. Create a schedule. After you've met with your travel agent, create a schedule with the due dates for each of the phases of your trip. This includes knowing when you need to have all of the traveler information to the agent, when they need copies of passports/IDs, and when down payments and final payments are due.

How to Book an Open Jaw Flight

Open-jaw flights are a great way to travel to two places without needing to waste time circling back to your original destination on the way home. They are also about the same price as a regular round-trip flight. So, they save you time and money!

Method 1

Traditional Method

1. Go to your favorite flight search engine.

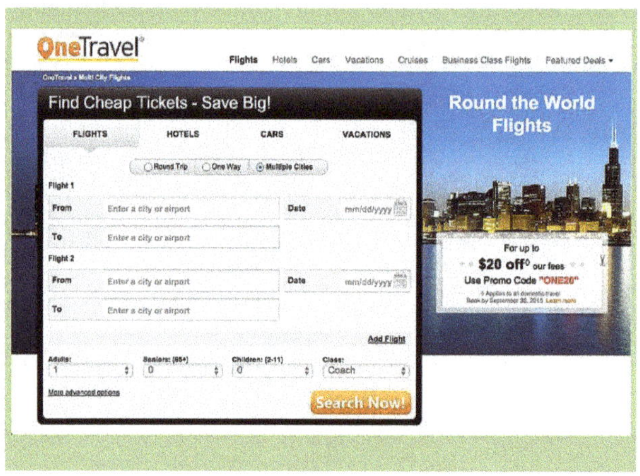

2. Look for the "multi-city" or "multiple destinations" link.

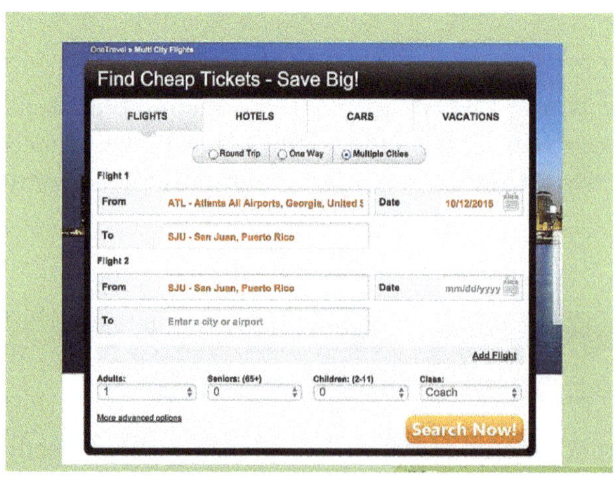

3. Enter your home airport as the "from airport" for the first leg, and the "to airport" for the second leg.

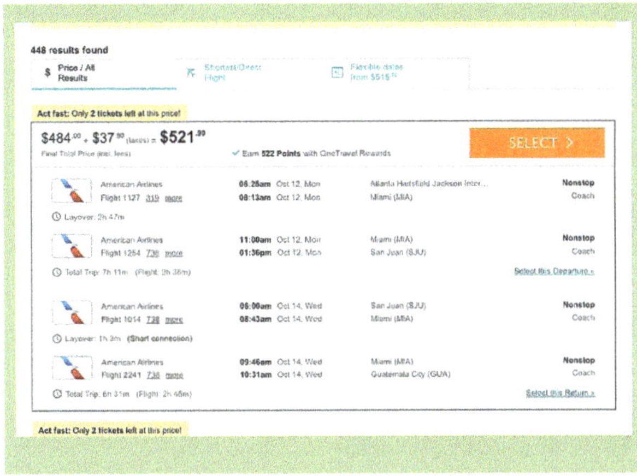

4. Pick one of your destinations and enter it as the "to airport" of the first leg. Use the other destination as the "from airport" of the second leg. Click the "search" or "find flights" button.

5. Repeat the search process but this time swap the order of visiting the two destinations. Sometimes one order will have better flights than the other.

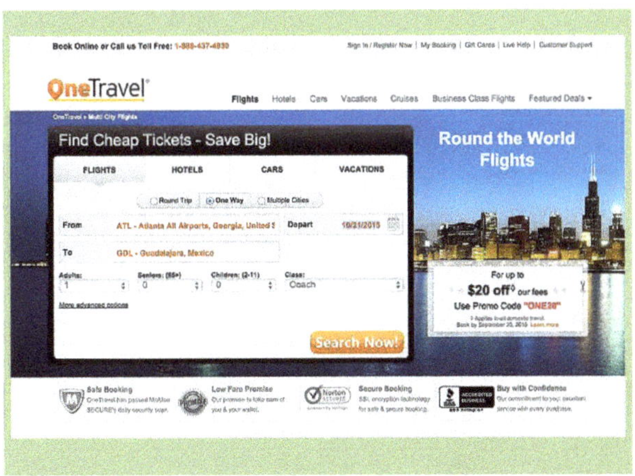

6. Do a separate, one-way search to figure out how to get between the two destinations. You could enter all three flights into the same search but this will often result in more expensive flight options.

7. If you are visiting more than two destinations, you'll have to try mixing and matching until you find the right combination of two destinations to serve as your first and last destination. In some cases, you can book another (inverted) open-jaw to form an "end-on-end" itinerary.

Method 2

Automated Method

1. Find a service to search for open jaw flights. Some web sites are designed specifically to handle optimizing trips across multiple destinations.

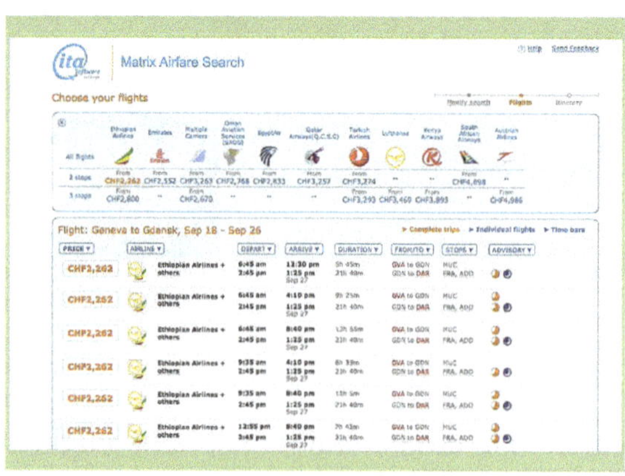

2. Enter your destinations. On this multi-destination site, you can typically enter the list of

places you'd like to visit into a simple form and then click search. The site will compute the optimal itinerary for visiting those places, incorporating open-jaws and one-way flights as appropriate.

How to Purchase Consolidator Airline Tickets

Consolidators are ticket brokers who negotiate airline ticket prices (primarily international tickets) directly with the airlines and sell them to travelers at discounted prices, sometimes at prices up to 70% lower than the airlines' published prices. Consolidator contracts are awarded to companies that show excellent selling records and big volumes. This topic explains how to purchase consolidator airline tickets, provides useful tips and lists some of the better known consolidators.

Steps

1. Plan your travel ahead of time but be flexible on exact dates and flights. If price is your number-one priority, booking consolidator airplane tickets can save you money.

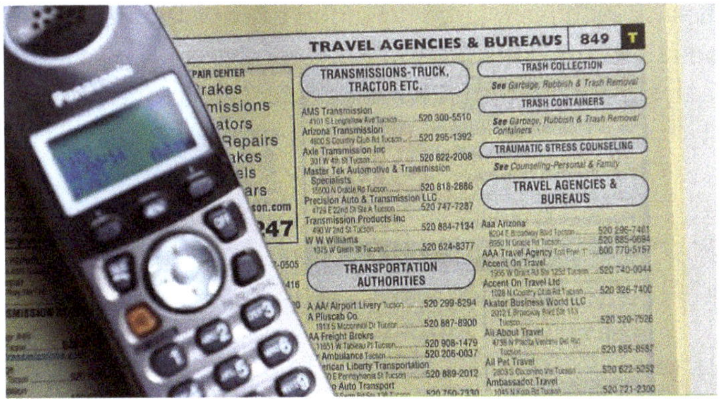

2. Work with a travel professional. A travel agent is the best way to purchase tickets from a reputable consolidator. Travel agents who deal with consolidator tickets will have a list of consolidators they work with on a consistent basis so they know who is reputable and who is not. Although they may add a slight mark-up to the ticket, the price you pay will be less than anywhere else you purchase the tickets. Plus, if you have a problem with flight delays or cancellations, you have a person to contact.

3. Examine the travel section of your local newspaper, especially the Sunday edition, for advertisements from airline ticket consolidators who sell to the public.

4. Go online. Although many travel sites advertise that they sell wholesale fares, only a few of them actually do. Each of these sites have a large selection of consolidator tickets and they handle the customer service on behalf of the consolidator so you have an advocate in case of a problem. If you use an online consolidator make sure you can contact the company off the Internet, in case of emergencies.

How to Redeem Credit Card Rewards

Many credit card programs offer rewards or perks to entice customers to apply for a particular card. The more often you use a card, the more reward points you can collect. You can redeem reward points for a variety of items, including concert tickets, airline miles, gift cards, and other products. When applying for a card, be sure to review the details of the contract to ensure that you understand how the program works. Each credit card company has different terms and conditions for their reward programs, and each company will offer different methods for cashing out your points. Understanding the most popular ways to redeem credit card points can help you select the right option.

Part 1

Learning How to Exchange your Credit Card Points

1. Review the rewards catalog. Your credit card company may provide you with a print or online rewards catalog. The catalog will typically detail the structure of the rewards program and will list the reward options available. Each reward will have a unique code and the required number of points needed to redeem it. After reviewing the catalog, call the customer service department or go online to redeem your selected reward.

- Be sure to have the reward code handy and check that you have accrued enough points to receive the desired reward. Your monthly credit card statement will list the number of reward points you have earned.

2. Call the card's customer service department. For help redeeming reward points, you can contact your credit card's customer service line. Most rewards programs will allow you to redeem your points over the phone. The representative can let you know your available point balance and what rewards are available to you. They can also answer any questions you may have about your point accumulation and how long it will take to receive your reward.

3. Redeem your rewards online. Most credit card companies will provide you with access to your credit card statements, reward options, and redemption choices on an online portal or mobile banking app. Once you have signed into your account, look for a section that references your credit card points, such as "Redeem My Rewards," or "Use My Points." Click through to this section to review and claim your reward.

- Collecting your rewards online is similar to a regular online shopping experience, where you browse through the items available and add them to your cart. Instead of supplying payment information during the check-out process, you will be able to easily complete the transaction by exchanging your reward points.

4. Complete a redemption form. Some reward programs will allow you to complete a redemption form, which you can then mail or fax to the credit card company. This form will ask that you provide a description of your selected reward along with the reward code, which can be found in the rewards catalog. The form can usually be found in your online or print rewards catalog.

- Be aware that it may take longer to receive your rewards when you use this redemption option.

5. Use your credit card to make purchases as usual. As you make purchases, you will accrue reward points for each dollar or other currency you spend. If you use your card for most purchases and pay off your bill in a timely manner, you can quickly accrue reward points. Be sure that you can pay off your credit card on time so you do not have to pay a late free.

Part 2

Selecting a Reward Option

1. Cash out your reward points. Sixty-one percent of cardholders elect to redeem their points by transferring them into a cash. Typically, a card will provide 2% cash back on your purchases, but many cards now have a rotating point system—some months you will earn double points while buying groceries with your card, and other months you may earn more when you use your card at particular gas stations.

- This complicated system may make it difficult to keep track of how many points you have accumulated and how much money you will receive. However, redeeming your points for cash is a great way to ensure that you can spend the money however you wish.

2. Use your points for gift cards. Gift cards are a great way to redeem your reward points. Credit

cards typically offer 1 cent for each point you accumulate. If your company offers gift cards for stores where you typically shop or would like to shop, this option may be the best for you.

- Some credit card companies have a limited selection of shops to choose from, which may not be helpful if you do not shop at those particular stores. Your credit card contract or catalog should detail your options for redeeming gift cards.

3. Elect to have your points transferred to a financial investment. There are a few credit cards that allow you to transfer your points into an a financial investment, a savings account, or an individual retirement account, or IRA. These cards often have excellent customer service as they are affiliated with particular financial institutions and brokerage firms, and the rewards percentage is usually higher than the average 1%. In addition, it makes contributing to your financial accounts easy.

4. Choose to spend your points on products. Many banks and credit card companies will allow you to log in to your online account and browse their online shop where your credit card points are your currency. This seems like a great option to finally snag a gadget or product you have had your eye on, but often the product price in the online shop is much more expensive than it is in a regular store. Research the product you want before redeeming it in the rewards shop.

5. Redeem your points for travel. Many reward options offer travelers the chance to translate points into discounted airline tickets, rental cars, and hotel stays. If you frequently travel, this may be a great option for you. However, there are only certain times when you can redeem these perks. If you try to book travel during a blackout time, you won't be able to redeem your credit card points. Be sure to ask your credit card company about their policy for booking travel with your reward points.

How to Convert Credit Card Points to Frequent Flyer Miles

Many credit card companies offer rewards points that can be exchanged for, or applied to, frequent flyer miles. The conversion process and rates will depend on your credit card terms. However, with the right strategies in place, you can usually earn heavily discounted or free flights to any destination.

Part 1

Earning Credit Card Points

1. Check your current credit card's rewards program. If you already have a credit card, check your

card agreement or your issuer's website to see whether you have a points reward program. This program allows you to earn points based on your purchases that can be redeemed for rewards like cash back, gift cards, or frequent flyer miles. Contact your card issuer if you are unsure if your card qualifies for this type of program.

2. Find a credit card with a frequent flyer mile reward program. If your current card doesn't offer points rewards or the chance to convert points to miles, you'll need to get a card that does. This type of reward is offered from almost all credit cards that offer points, but some options are better than others. Search online to locate cards that allow you to transfer points to miles at a good rate. For example, the following rewards programs allows you to transfer points to miles at a rate of 1 to 1:

- American Express Member Rewards. This is available to all American Express cardholders.
- Citi Thank You. This is available on Citi Thank You cards and others.
- Chase Ultimate Rewards. Access this program by signing up for a Chase Sapphire Preferred or Ink Plus for Business card.
- There may be other cards offering a good transfer rate that are a better fit to your spending habits and financial situation. Research terms for several different cards before making a decision.

3. Take advantage of any signup bonuses. Many credit cards offer signup bonuses that immediate-

ly credit your rewards account a large number of points if you reach a certain spending milestone within a set time period. In many cases, this can be a significant number of points, perhaps 50,000 or 100,000.

- However, you should avoid simply spending to reach this limit, as this might cause you to overspend. Instead, make sure that the spending milestone is in line with your regular spending patterns.

4. Make qualifying purchases. Points must be built up by making qualifying purchases on your credit card. The qualifications for a qualified purchase vary between card issuers, so check your card agreement to see what you should use your card for. For example, some point rewards programs offer a flat points rate for all purchases. However, others reward certain purchases, like gas or entertainment, at a higher rate. Others might have a rotating high rewards category each month.

- Wherever possible, put qualifying purchases on your credit card. This will help you earn points without changing your spending habits.

5. Build up a sizable points balance. Even with signup bonuses and frequent credit card purchases, building up a points balance will take time. Many flights you will want to take after converting your points will end up costing upwards of 30,000 miles. For example, a trip to Europe from the US might cost 50,000 to 60,000 points. This means you'll have to take the time to build up a points balance before they will become truly useful.

Part 2

Determining Conversion Eligibility

1. Locate reward program details. Request a copy of your points program information from your credit card company by calling customer support. This information will also be available online through your card issuer's website. Reward programs typically vary. Different credit cards have different guidelines and restrictions and you should know the specifics of the program to which you belong.

- Figure out how, specifically, you can convert your points. You may need to call, but in many cases you can go through the whole process online.

2. Call your credit card company and speak to a representative. Confirm or clarify any details regarding the reward program you don't understand. Make sure that you have all of the information you need to make an informed decision about the best way to use your frequent flyer miles.

- Ask about any changes to the rewards program, as these can happen without notice and may affect your miles conversion.

3. Confirm the points to miles conversion rate. This will depend on your card and the chosen fre-

quent flyer miles program. For instance, for some credit cards, 1 point is equivalent to 1 mile. If you have 20,000 points then you will be eligible for 20,000 miles. American Express converts 1,000 rewards points to 750 Delta SkyMiles, while Citi converts 1,000 rewards points to 1,000 Advantage miles.

- Transfer your points to the frequent flyer program that offers the best conversion rates.

4. Know if your credit card points or flyer miles have an expiration date. Most points expire within a set timeframe if they go unused. You will want to convert your points to miles and use them before they expire. If your points are expiring and you have no chance to use them, consider giving them to a friend or family member. You can also donate them to charity in most cases.

5. Check your mile-conversion details. Look out for any regulations or blackout dates that may be imposed upon your miles. Some companies do not allow travel on certain days, times of the year, or to certain destinations. Take notice of restrictions on dates, airlines and destinations.

Part 3

Booking Your Flight

1. Create a frequent flyer account online with an airline that is approved by your credit card company. Some companies require that you sign up for a frequent flyer account, while others will apply a travel credit directly to your card account. Investigate flight prices in miles as well. Trip prices may vary widely between airlines, so be sure to check several different ones to find the best deal.

- For example, one airline might offer a specific trip for 70,000 miles, whereas another might have the same trip for 50,000.

2. Plan ahead. It may take weeks or months to redeem your credit card points for frequent flyer miles that you can use to book a flight. However, some rewards programs allow you to convert points instantly and many of them will make the conversion within a week. Check the terms of your rewards program or call customer service to get an idea of how much time you need to allocate for this process.

- Try booking in off-times for your destination, as this will make your travel cheaper. For example, don't try to fly to Mexico during the winter holidays, as flights will be more expensive.

3. Book your flight with an airline that is approved by your credit card company. Not all airlines are valid with frequent flyer rewards. Make sure your points have definitely been converted and you have received a travel credit before booking your flight.

- You should also transfer miles to airlines you have transferred miles to or flown with in the past. This will allow you to build up miles with that airline and earn greater rewards.
- Miles may be used on all airlines within the same alliance (a group of airlines). The main alliances are:
    - Star Alliance: United, US Airways, Swiss Air, Lufthansa, and others.
    - One World: American Airways, British Airways, Iberia, and others.
    - SkyTeam: Delta, Air France, Korean, and others.

4. Input your frequent flyer account information when booking a flight online. There will usually be a field asking for your frequent flyer account number. Have this information on hand. If you run into trouble booking using rewards point, call the airlines to speak to a representative. They will be able to help you complete the transaction.

How to use Credit Card Rewards Points

Credit card rewards points have become a central component of many Americans' financial planning. With so many companies in competition with one another, you have a lot to choose from.

Knowing how you will use a card as well as its rewards up front is a part of a balanced budget. Make sure you sign up for a card after weighing all its fees and perks with a detailed cost-benefit analysis. You may be able to use your points for expenditures you make every week, or even tuck away some money in savings.

Method 1

Maximizing Rewards Possibilities

1. Go for a smart signup bonus. There are hundreds of credit cards you could pick. This means that they are all competing with each other to get you to sign. Look at the different sign-up bonuses to see who will fix you up with the most rewards possibilities up front.

- For example, a good signup bonuses might give you high points or airline miles in the first several months for relatively little money spent. If the cash equivalent of what they are offering you is at least 10% of the amount you spent, it's a pretty good deal.
- Stay away from cards that offer you a tempting sum of rewards points up front, but then pull the rug out from under you. This is especially dangerous if the sign-up bonus peters out long before your ability to cancel the card without incurring a hefty fee.

2. Review your rewards points system. This process will help you determine which purchases will earn you the highest number of rewards points. If you have a steady income, you may want to open

a few different cards for different spending. You will simply have more companies to pay the same amount of money at the end of the month.

- For example, if gas station purchases offer higher rewards than purchases you make at a retail store, charge all your gas station purchases to that credit card. Find another credit card that rewards you for retail store purchases.

3. Redeem your rewards points before they expire. Rewards points are an artificial currency created by your credit card company. They aren't susceptible to the same laws of nature of real money. This means your credit card company can set and expiration date, and your rewards vanish in thin air. Know your expiration dates, and get whatever you can if you find yourself approaching one.

- Using your rewards points sooner rather than later is a good policy. This way you can plan how you use it rather than potentially having to scramble to figure out something last minute.

4. Check your rewards points system often. Most rewards systems include the stipulation that the credit card company can amend the contract at any time. They may notify you, but they may not. It usually isn't drastic – maybe that flight to Lincoln costs 4,500 points instead of 4,000. However, you should make yourself aware when this happens. You don't want to plan the yearly trip to Nebraska only to find out you have to pay cash when you weren't planning to.

- This is another good reason to plan on using rewards points quickly. Some credit card companies use the stick-and-carrot approach to rewards points – they want to keep you saving up points without ever cashing in.

5. Cancel if necessary. Sometimes, the cards with the best signup bonuses have no intention of letting you continue to fork in the rewards. Check out your contract, and do a cost-benefit analysis to see if it is worth the fee to cancel early. If you will save yourself money by cancelling the card, pull the plug.

Method 2

Using Rewards for Travel

1. Look into travel rewards. Many credit card companies offer great airline and hotel discounts for rewards points. Each credit card will have its own rewards policies, so you should check with several companies. Look at the policies and read some online reviews to see which one best fits your needs and interests.

- Some credit cards are better for domestic flights, and some are better for international flights. Look into the rewards points conversion rates for each credit card to see which suits your needs.

2. Check if the rewards can also be used on hotels. Some credit card companies only book travel tickets, like for airlines and trains. You may be able to pay for a whole trip by using your points on the airfare as well as the hotel. This is an attractive perk, but don't sign up for a card that has lower rewards exchange rates due to a wider range of rewards possibilities.

3. Look for restrictions on travel. Blackout dates are used by airline companies and hotels to keep customers using rewards points from booking flights on popular days. For example, you may not be able to trade in your airline points for the Easter weekend trip to see the family. If this is important to you, make sure to choose a credit card with no blackout dates on travel rewards.

4. Look for a credit card that lets you earn airline miles for the trips you take. Some even let you earn double miles for those points. Another popular option is to actually convert the rewards

points into airline miles. That means that you don't directly get a trip for your rewards points, but can apply them with an approved airline any way you wish.

5. Compare the cost of the trip with the cash equivalent. The cost of the flight may be drastically less than the cash equivalent of your points. For example, there may be If you can use the points in a more lucrative way, opt out of the plane ticket. It may be that you still need to pay a small amount for the trip, but the rewards points get you a pretty good discount.

6. Plan ahead. Schedule your trips and reservations prior to the expiration date on your credit card. Some rewards points may not be honored if your card has expired. Consult with your credit card company to verify the rules surrounding making plans and reservations for trips and vacations.

Method 3

Turning Rewards Into Money

1. Get a cash kickback. The easiest way to turn your rewards points into value is by trading them in

for cash. Check the rates before you decide to do this. Even though it would be money in your pocket, a gift card may be a much better deal. Make sure a gas card or supermarket gift card wouldn't give you a much better return for your points.

2. Reinvest in savings. Many credit card companies allow you to route your rewards points right back into a savings account. This could be a college fund, a retirement savings account – even your 401k in some cases. This may not be the sexiest way to use your rewards points, but it may be the best choice in the long run. Putting some money away for a rainy day is never a bad idea, and this way you don't even have to divert cash from your checking account to do it.

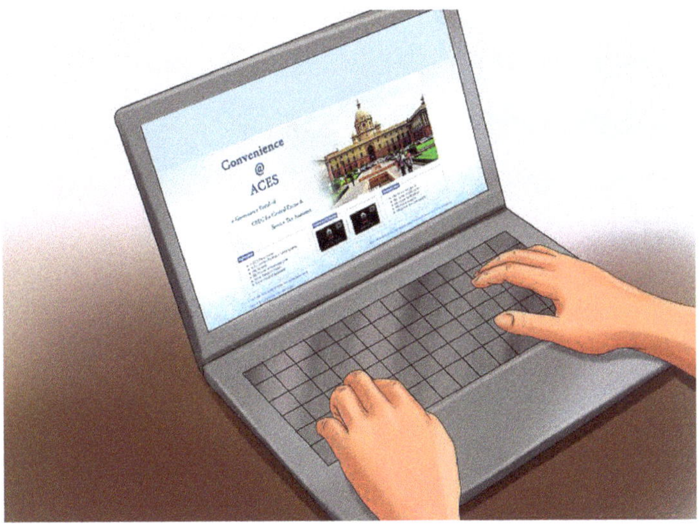

3. Use your rewards to pay taxes. Many credit card companies now give you the chance to apply your rewards directly to your taxes. If this gives you a chance to keep a considerable amount of money in your pocket, go for it. As always, check the cash equivalent.

- A factor to keep in mind is the way you are allowed to pay taxes. Most credit cards require you to use an online tax filing service. These always have additional fees, which should factor into your cost-benefit analysis.

4. Trade them in for gift cards. Some credit card companies have partnerships or agreements with businesses that enable them to offer you tempting gift card values. In some cases, this greatly exceeds the cash amount you could trade your points in for. Make sure you do a careful cost-benefit analysis of the cash value of the gift card and your other rewards possibilities.

- The best gift cards to opt for are companies that you already regularly use. Gas cards, supermarket cards, and other essentials are a great option because that is money you would spend no matter what. But if you really want to treat yourself to a new rod and reel at the sporting goods store, go for it!

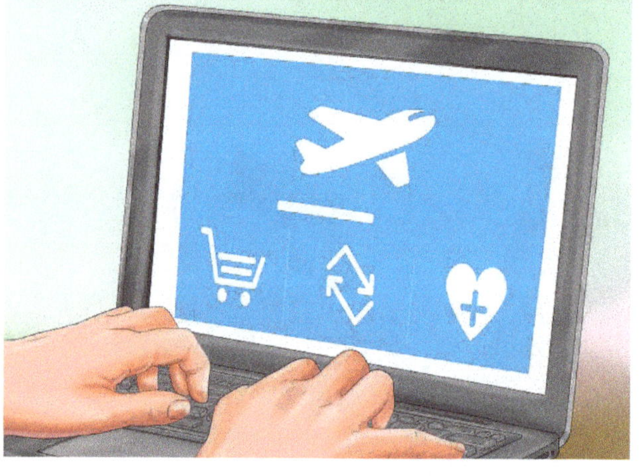

5. Donate your surplus rewards points. If you don't see a way to use your rewards points except by trading for something you don't need, consider donating them. Charities use rewards points in a variety of ways. Your points can be as good as cash for many organizations. Even though this doesn't qualify as a tax deductible donation, it will help those in need.

- Some charities trade donated rewards points for specific items like travel, just as you might. This enables, for instance, grieving family members or cancer patients to book flights they can't afford.
- Other charities are able to trade the rewards points for a cash amount and apply the money how they see fit.

How to Buy Airline Tickets with Credit Card Reward Miles

One of the greatest benefits of credit cards is earning rewards when you spend with the card. Miles that can be redeemed for airline tickets are a common reward. The process for buying tickets with reward miles may vary by credit card company, but the basic process is simple enough. You should learn about your specific credit card company's reward system. You'll also learn some ways to accrue as many miles as you can.

Method 1

Redeeming your Points

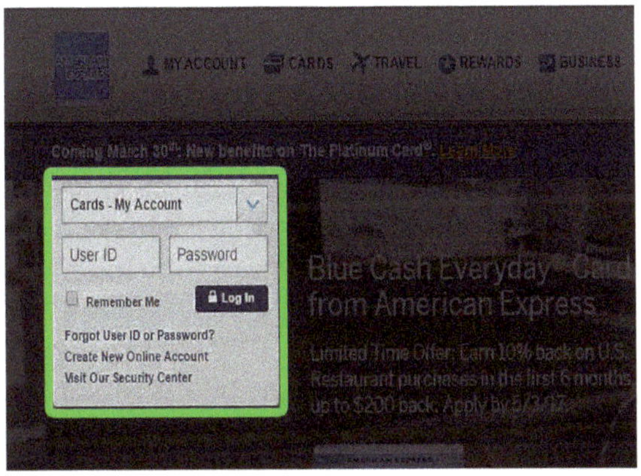

1. Create an online account for your credit card. Most rewards programs use an online account to redeem miles or points. Visit your credit card company's site to set up an online account. American Express, for example, has a sign in box in the top left corner. Be sure to create a secure password that you will remember.

- Online accounts also let you track your spending on the card and may even allow for paying your monthly balance.

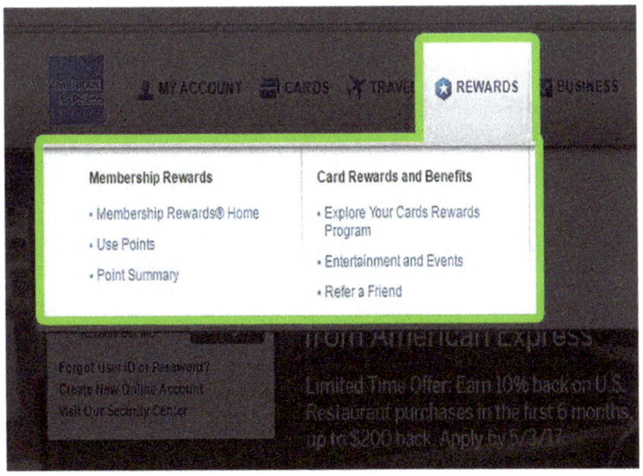

2. Check your points balance online. Most credit card account sites will have a "Points" or "Bal-

ance" tab, which will show your current reward miles or points. After checking your balance, look for a tab that says "Redeem" or "Use Points" or something similar.

- If you prefer to book reward travel by phone, then look in your credit card rewards information to find the phone number or extension that is dedicated to award travel. Try to prepare your travel date and destination options ahead of time for expediency.

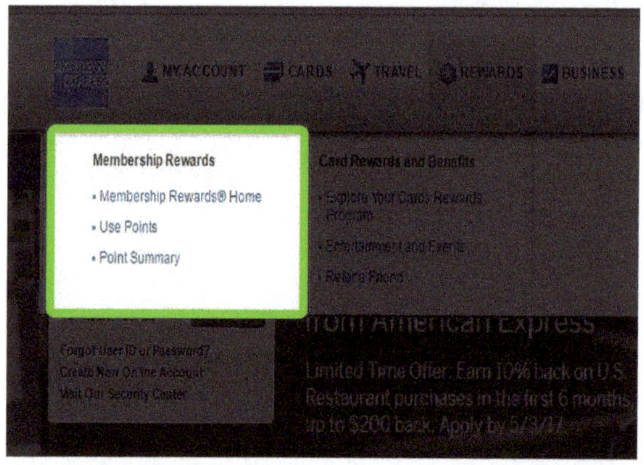

3. Choose a flight through your credit card site. Your credit card account should offer the option to search for flights that are purchasable with reward miles. Most credit cards will have limitations based on airlines, dates of travel, and destination, so you may have to search a little while and possibly compromise to choose a flight that works for you.

- Your card may offer the option to use some of the points rather than all of them. For example, if you are purchasing a $400 ticket, you might use just enough points to pay for half of the price.
- During the payment stage, look for an option about redeeming points. There should be a box where you can input how many points you want to use, or perhaps a checkbox that says "Use points for whole price," or something similar.

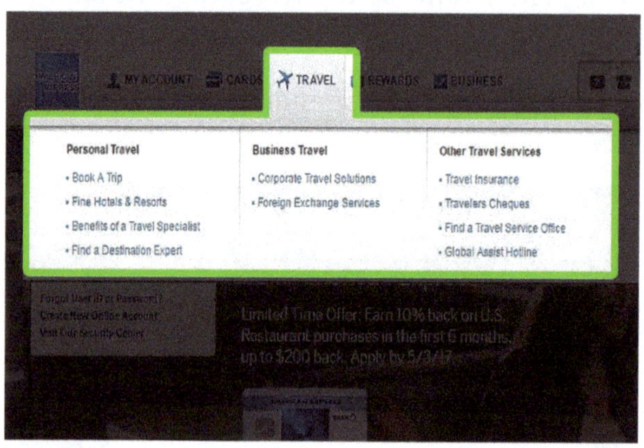

4. Search for flights on an airline website. Booking directly through an airline often gives you the best prices because there may be lower overhead or booking fees. If you have a card that is affiliated with that airline, you'll be able to log in with your member number or input it during the payment stage after you choose your flight.

- You can also use frequent flier miles that you've earned with that specific airline.

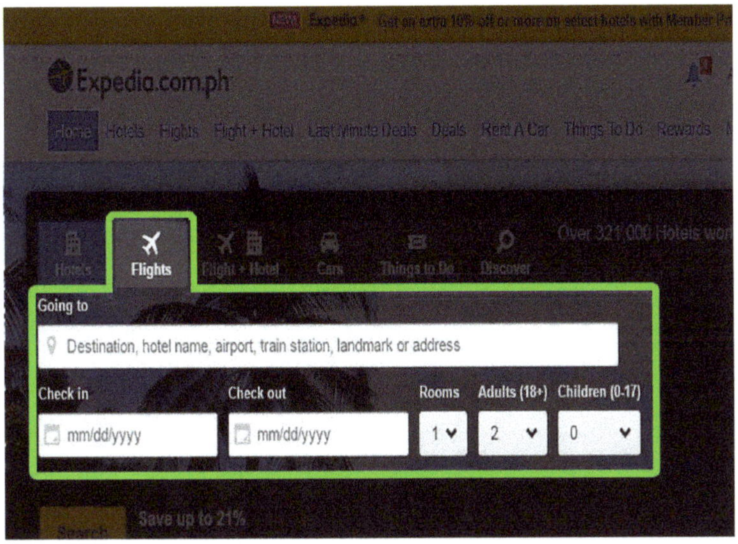

5. Use a flight aggregator to select a ticket. You can book a ticket through a flight aggregator such as Expedia or Orbitz. You are able to use credit card rewards points provided that you have a credit card that is affiliated with those sites. For example, Expedia uses Citi Thank You Points and Orbitz pairs with Visa.

- Some aggregators may allow you to use a non-affiliated card. If that option is available, you will find it once you choose flights and are inputting your payment information. You may not be able to use reward points from a non-affiliated card.
- Many aggregators also have their own rewards points programs that allow you to earn books when you repeatedly book through their site. This can be a good way to get the most of using reward points.

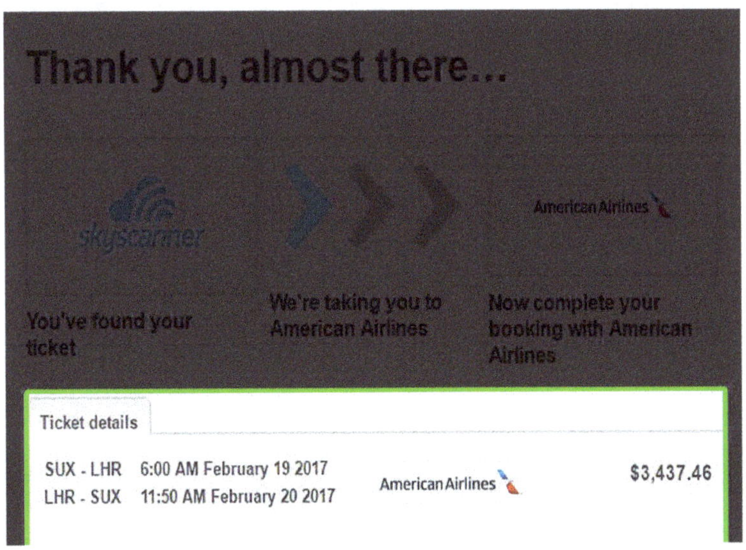

6. Select the ticket that fits you best. You'll often want to choose the cheapest option, but amenities and flight dates will also come into play. Choose based on your preferred airline, the dates that work best for you, or seat and cabin preferences.

- Once you have selected your ticket(s), the site will automatically move you onto the payment stage and you'll be asked to input your information.

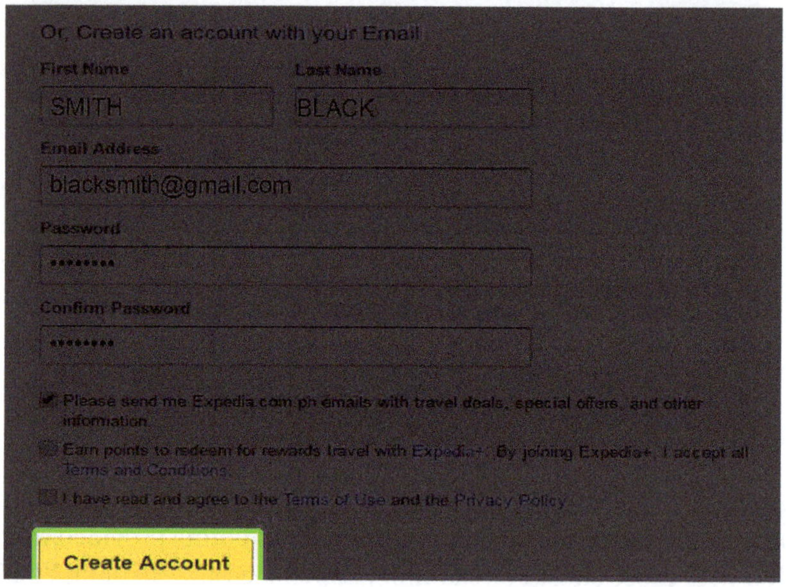

7. Input your information. Each credit card, airline, or flight aggregator site may offer slightly different payment options. When you get to the payment stage, you may have to log into airline or aggregator accounts if you have not already. Type in frequent flier information if you are asked and rewards member information if available.

- You will most likely only be able to use rewards points from the card that you input to pay for the ticket with.

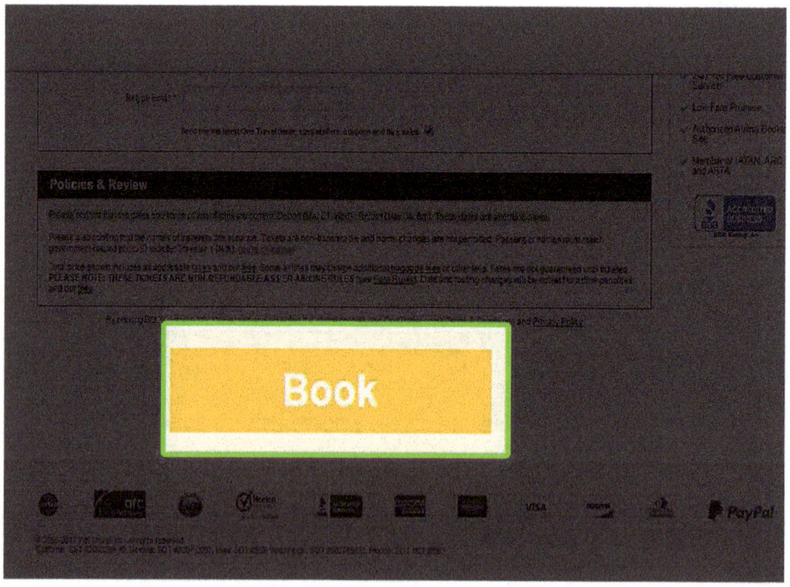

8. Finalize your ticket purchase. Once all of your information is inputted, you will be asked to make a final confirmation that all of the information you typed in is corrected. Check everything carefully.

Method 2

Using your Rewards System

1. Ask your credit card company for detailed rewards information. If you are planning to sign up for a new card, learn as much as you can about the rewards system. If you have the card already, contact customer service and request any information they have about their rewards program.

- Be sure to find out what purchases are eligible for earning rewards. You may be surprised by some of the restrictions.

2. Be aware of how card cancellations affect your points. If your credit card is paired with an airline or a hotel, then your points are most likely earned with that company rather than the bank. Cards that are not paired with another company will only earn points with the issuing bank or credit company.

- Points earned through a second company (like an airline or hotel) are safe when you cancel, but points earned through a bank will be lost.

3. Check the value of each mile (or point) you earn. Earned miles or points may differ in value from one credit card company to the next. Ask your credit card company directly to find out exactly what your miles are worth. You can also look for websites that list point values from various credit cards.

- Many credit card miles are worth 1 cent. This means that if you have 40,000, you can redeem them for a ticket that costs up to $400.

Method 3

Accruing Miles

1. Open a new credit card account. Many credit cards offer a sign on bonus when you start a new account. Even if you don't need another credit card, sign up for one and earn those initial points. You don't have to spend money on that specific card.

- This can be especially useful if you get a card that is paired with an airline that you already have a card or frequent flyer account with.

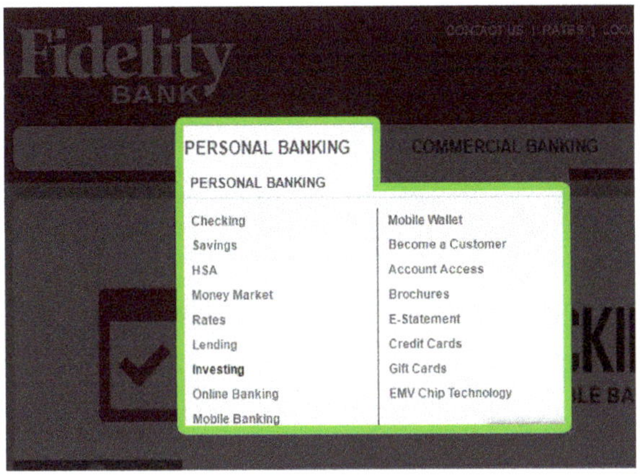

2. Start an investment account. Many credit cards partner with brokerage firms so you earn points when you invest money through those firms. Fidelity is one company that has this type of partnership with American, United, and Delta Airlines.

- You may earn points each time you deposit money into those investment accounts. If you are not comfortable investing, make sure you know what is required of you before starting an investment account.

3. Shape your spending around earning miles. As you continue to earn miles, begin to change your spending habits to earn as many points as you can. If shopping online earns you more points than shopping in the store, do it. If certain restaurants earn you points and others don't, eat at the restaurants that earn points more.

- Some people make it a hobby to search out the best miles earning options that are available. If travel is important you, develop a spending strategy that earns you the most miles possible.

How to Get an Upgrade to First Class

Have you always wanted to fly first class or business class, but just never had the money? Or maybe you got a huge bonus just before your vacation, and want to upgrade a flight already booked. Well, hang on to your carry-on: here are a few things you can do to get yourself placed into those plush, spacious seats!

Method 1

Methods with A Higher Success Rate

1. Buy an upgrade. This is by far the easiest, most sure-fire way to get an upgrade. However, unless you fly often with the airline and have earned elite status, it's also the most expensive way to enjoy the perks of first class.

2. Become a frequent flier. Airlines categorize their customers based on how often they fly—or more to the point, how much they spend.

- At 50k miles a year, you are in the middle of the "elite" zone, a position that makes you important to the airline. You'll be rewarded with various perks along the way—from quick check-ins, to bonus miles, to first-class upgrades.
- If you don't normally travel a lot for business or pleasure, consider "mileage running." This is the process of finding cheap, long flights and taking them whenever possible. The destination is not important—only the distance. A good rule of thumb for determining if a mileage run is worth it is if the price-per-mile cost is $.02 or below. Check out online resources such as Farecompare for prices and opportunities.

- You might also consider whether you fly frequently enough to maintain elite status.

3. Check in at the airport kiosk. Arrive at the airport a couple hours early, and check in using the airline's kiosk. You will be able to modify your seat assignment as available, and if there are any first-class seats available, you may be able to purchase an upgrade at a significantly reduced cost.

4. Check in early. When there is one upgrade available and two elite flyers are requesting it, all else being equal: the one who checks in first gets it. You must have elite status with the airline for this to work.

5. Get bumped! Take advantage of opportunities that arise during the normal course of travel. All airlines over-book flights, and sometimes, when they least expect it, *everybody* shows up for the

flight. When that happens, they have to find people willing to be bumped from that flight. That could be you!

- If the flight is very overbooked, your bargaining position is strong. Approach the gate agent, and be as genuinely charming and sympathetic as you can be. Ask them if they would consider rebooking you in return for an upgrade voucher in addition to whatever other incentives they might be offering.
- This will be more likely to work if you don't have checked baggage, which would entail much more work on the part of the airlines in order to bump you.

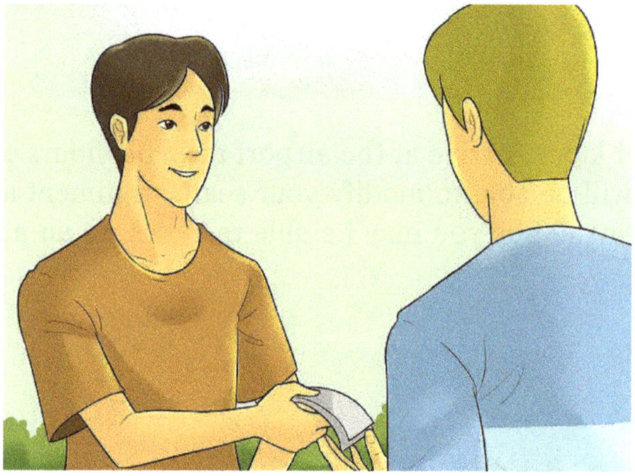

6. Find discounted tickets. Some airlines have relaxed upgrade policies for full-fare coach tickets. You may also have friends who have upgrade vouchers they may be willing to sell.

7. Plan long-term. If you are a regular flier, are considering doing mileage runs, and are planning a big trip that you want to enjoy in first-class style, you can also purchase miles directly from the airlines.

- Visit your airline's website, and locate the "Purchase Miles" page, generally located in the frequent-flier part of the site.
- Enter your account number, and how many miles you wish to purchase.

8. Book directly with the airline. When you book directly with the airline, there is the possibility of also adding an OSI (Other Significant Information) notation to your record.

- Based on that, ask about the possibility of an upgrade to first class. If you are a travel agent, travel writer, event planner, or captain of industry, it certainly won't hurt your chances.

9. Buy a full fare coach ticket and ask for a first class seat. Many airlines have a fare code that automatically grants first class privileges, but you have to ask. Call the airline directly and ask them how much a coach class ticket with first class seating privilege will cost. This will be much less than a first class ticket. Be careful though, like most coach tickets it will probably be non-refundable.

10. Shop around. Reward airlines that have reasonable prices for business-class travel. As with any

airline, if you fly frequently, they appreciate your business, and a struggling upstart might appreciate your business even more.

Method 2

Methods with a Lower Success Rate

1. Book with a Travel Agent. Agents are routinely allotted a certain number of upgrade vouchers. This will not come free but you can persuade your agent for a business class flight voucher if they have any available.

- If you're not a frequent user of a particular travel agent, they have very little incentive to try to get you an upgrade. Whatever discretionary vouchers they may have will most certainly go to the people who have contributed the most to their agency.
- Travel agents have much less input regarding your status now than they used to. Your seat assignments are done via computer now, and computers don't take into account notes that a travel agent may have added to your record. Computers are quite content to simply count the miles and use your earned status.

2. Use a mileage broker. Mileage brokers buy mileage from frequent fliers, and resell those miles to other travelers.

- This is very risky. Airlines have very strict policies *against* buying frequent flier miles from a 3rd party. If they catch you doing this, you will likely lose your ticket, and you may also lose *all* your miles, earned or purchased.
- As a result of strict policies, brokers are hard to come by.

3. Ask the ticket counter agent nicely. This will almost never work. In most cases, on most airlines, the ticket agent is not authorized to upgrade. Only the manager is, so if there is only one person at the ticketing counter, you are talking to them.

- You will most likely need to use miles to get your upgrade. However, you might be able to ask the ticket counter agent to kindly add a code to your ticket. That signifies to the gate agent that you are potentially eligible for an upgrade.
- You have a better chance with international airlines.

4. If you were late because of a partner airline, make sure the airline is aware of that: it is their fault and they need to fix it. Both airlines need to be on the same E-ticket number, so both airlines are responsible for getting you to your destination. If they can't get you to your destination on time, that's a great time to ask—as nicely as possible—for another flight, plus an upgrade voucher for your troubles.

5. If you happen to be a travel agent, show your Iata or ARC ID. Again, if and only if seats are available will an airline offer a free upgrade and even though a travel agent might have some pull (this pull ended in the late 90's), you always have to assume that frequent flyer status will help more than just travel agent status. If you have both, you will only improve your chances of an upgrade. It certainly does not hurt to try.

6. Ask a flight attendant for an upgrade if you see a seat available. Typically flight attendants never upgrade passengers and simply asking for an upgrade is not going to work. However, there are legitimate reasons why a flight attendant might upgrade you. Here are a few:

- A problem with your seat. In some cases where your seat has malfunctioned and you cannot comfortably sit there, i.e. a seat-belt problem or the seat will not stay in the up position, the flight attendant will make an attempt to find you another seat. If no other seats are available in coach yet space is available in first, you may be moved to first class. However, this is a *very* rare occurrence, and you should never try to purposely break your seat. Also note that if there is an elite flier in coach, they may get the bump to first class, and you would take the elite member's old seat.
- Choose Seats at the bulkhead, where families with children get seated. This can result in an upgrades if they need your seat, which they often do.
- A problem with a fellow passenger. If by chance you are sitting next to a passenger and

you have a legitimate complaint such as harassment, the flight attendant can, at their discretion, move you to another seat. If there are only seats available in first class, up you go.

7. Get to know the airline employees you deal with regularly. Do you fly in and out of a certain airport regularly? If so, getting to know the agents you deal with often yields rewards. When a delay occurs, you could be the first person they think of to upgrade, or at least put to on a better flight. They will appreciate your loyalty and friendship, and will accommodate you accordingly.

8. Look the part. Dress like a business executive and at the very least, business casual. This means no jeans, athletic shoes or wear or other very casual attire. Looking like a first class passenger helps. Airlines are more willing to upgrade passengers who look as though they will fit in with those who willingly paid the extra money. You may also be able to get a seat in business class.

- Be aware that most upgrades are not based on looks, but on status. If you don't travel frequently but look like an MBA all-star, and the choice is between you and a sloppy-looking but extremely well-traveled NBA all-star, your Gucci's just won't count.

How to Change a Flight Reservation

If you are traveling by plane and find that you need to change the date or time of your flight, there will be fees to pay. Sometimes, changing reservations cannot be avoided, however. Be prepared with your original itinerary before you make changes to your flight. If you booked your original flight online, you might be able to make changes to the reservation online. You might find it more helpful to talk to an agent who can help you make the necessary changes and answer any questions. Change a flight reservation by accessing your reservation online, or calling an agent with the airline or travel agency you used.

Steps

1. Gather any confirmations numbers, receipts or other documentation with your flight information on it.

2. Check to see if your flights are nonrefundable. If your tickets are nonrefundable, expect to pay an administrative change fee of around $150, plus the difference in the ticket price.

3. Figure out what changes need to be made. Whether you need to depart or arrive on a different day or at a different time, be ready to share this information when you go online or talk to an agent.

4. Pull up the website of the airline you used to make the reservation. If you used an online travel site such as Expedia or Orbitz, you will need to call them.

5. Log in to the airline's website if you are a registered user, or have a frequent flyer number that will identify you.

- Sign in as a guest if you do not have log in details. Most airlines will still allow you to make changes without registering with the website.

6. Look for a tab that says "My Reservations" or "Change Flights." Click on that tab.

- Type in the required information, such as your last name, confirmation number or flight number. Some airlines might ask you to verify the credit card you used to book the ticket.

7. Select the flights you want to change. You will be able to search for new flights.

8. Choose new flights and click on the button that says "Continue."

- Review the summary of your changes. You should be told whether additional charges or refunds apply, and how much those are. Click "Continue" or "Make Changes" in order to confirm your new flights.

9. Pay any additional charges or fees with a credit card on the payment screen.

10. Wait for your confirmation, and print it out. You have successfully changed your flight reservation.

Changing a Flight Reservation by Phone

1. Locate contact information for the airline or travel agency that you used to book your flight.

2. Familiarize yourself with new flights that might work for you before you call. This will save you time.

- Look for new flights online, or use the automated service when you call the airline.

3. Provide the agent who answers your call with your name, confirmation number and original itinerary.

4. Explain the changes that you need to make, and if you have other flights in mind, share those with the agent.

5. Be patient while the agent makes the changes you have requested on his or her end.

6. Pay any additional charges and fees that apply to the new reservation. You will need to provide a credit or debit card number. Some airlines or agencies may be able to process the payment using a bank account.

7. Ask to have your new itinerary emailed or faxed to you. You have successfully changed your flight reservation.

How to Get Airline Compensation for Canceled Flights

When an airline cancels your flight, it may be more than simply inconvenient – especially if you're traveling for reasons other than leisure. Unfortunately, U.S. law doesn't require airlines to compensate passengers for the cancellation of domestic flights. If you're flying internationally, you may be legally entitled to compensation, but not without navigating a complex web of foreign and international law. Regardless, there are still ways to get airline compensation for canceled flights if you are persistent and do a little planning before you buy your tickets.

Method 1

Negotiating with the Airline

1. Determine if any international laws apply. Although U.S. law doesn't require airlines to compensate travelers for canceled domestic flights, you may be entitled to compensation for international flights.

- For example, Article 19 of an international treaty called the Warsaw Convention requires airlines to compensate passengers for any direct costs caused by a delay or cancellation, such as transportation, food, and accommodations.
- The European Union also has regulations regarding airline compensation for cancelled flights, provided the cancellation was due to something within the carrier's flight such as overbooking.

2. Check the airline's rules and policies. Even if compensation isn't required by law, many airlines have their own corporate policies allowing some manner of compensation for canceled flights.

- Keep in mind that full-service airlines are more likely to offer compensation for canceled flights than their no-frills, budget counterparts.
- Typically, the airline will offer to rebook you on the next available flight. However, this may cause complications if the flight doesn't leave for several hours or even days after the flight on which you were initially scheduled – particularly if you have an appointment at your destination or need to catch a connecting flight.
- Some airlines have a policy of reimbursing you for expenses you incurred for food or lodging as a result of a flight cancellation, but you must submit receipts and other information to the airline after the fact.

3. Contact the airline's customer service department. You should be able to find a phone number or website for customer service issues on your purchase confirmation, ticket, or boarding pass.

- You may get a more favorable response from the customer service line than you do from the employee at the ticket counter in the airport. That employee has to deal with potentially every person on your flight, while the customer service representative likely is working under less stressful conditions.
- Use facts to back up your argument that the canceled flight is more than a mere inconvenience for you, but avoid exaggerating or making something up to make your situation sound more dire.
- Keep in mind that if the airline does agree to compensate you, it likely will ask for proof of whatever loss you claim to have suffered.
- Take detailed notes during your phone call, including the date and time of your call and the names of any representatives with whom you speak.

4. Put your request in writing. Conducting your negotiations in writing provides you with proof of any promises that are made on the airline's behalf.

- If you are offered compensation by a telephone representative, write a letter as soon as possible detailing the conversation and the compensation offered. Include copies of any documents, receipts, or other information you were told to provide.
- Many airlines such as United also will provide a verification letter for you upon your re-

quest, which you can use as proof your flight was canceled. This letter may help you mitigate damages suffered as a result of any appointments or reservations you have to postpone or change as a result of your canceled flight.

5. Follow up with your request. Even if the airline has no corporate policy or legal requirement to compensate you for a canceled flight, persistence can pay off.

- If a reasonable amount of time has passed and the airline has refused your request for compensation or hasn't responded, look for the name of a director or manager to whom you can direct your future correspondence.
- You might also consider filing a complaint with the U.S. Department of Transportation (DOT). Since U.S. law doesn't require airline compensation for canceled flights, this likely won't get you much further, but the complaint will be passed on to the airline.
- To record a complaint about airline service with the DOT, you can call 202-366-2220. A DOT agent will return your call during regular business hours. You also can use the DOT's web form or write a letter and send it to Aviation Consumer Protection Division, C-75, U.S. Department of Transportation, 1200 New Jersey Ave, S.E., Washington, DC 20590.

Method 2

Using Credit Card Benefits

1. Check your credit card agreement. Many credit cards provide travel insurance as a benefit to cardholders who purchase plane tickets using that card.

- While many travel-oriented credit products offer travel insurance that provides compensation for expenses directly incurred as a result of a canceled flight, the coverage amounts and restrictions vary significantly. For example, some of these policies provide protection for the cardholder only, not members of your family who may have been traveling with you.
- Ideally, you should check the protections offered by your credit cards before you book your trip so you can use the card that provides the greatest level of protection in the event something goes wrong.
- While a few credit card companies do provide compensation for canceled flights, these policies most frequently cover accidents and loss or damage to luggage.

2. Contact customer service. Typically you can take advantage of any travel benefits provided by your credit card company by calling the customer service number on the back of your credit card.

- If you had to sign up separately for travel insurance benefits from your credit card company, there may be a separate phone number for you to call.
- Keep in mind that some of the cards require an additional sign-up process or fees to activate these benefits. This typically must be done before you purchase your tickets or go on your trip.

3. Explain your situation. Tell the customer service representative what happened to you and confirm the situation is covered by your cardholder benefits.

- Credit card companies that cover the costs of a delay, cancellation, or trip interruption typically only do so under certain circumstances such as weather or equipment failure. If your flight was canceled for some reason other than those covered by your credit card's policy, don't expect any compensation.

- You may need to submit a verification letter from the airline stating the reason your flight was canceled.
- Find out from the customer service representative what information and documentation is required for your claim to be processed, as well as any deadlines your credit card company may have for filing a claim.

4. Submit your claim. Follow your credit card company's guidelines to claim reimbursement or other compensation for your canceled flight.

- Typically the credit card company will only reimburse expenses you paid using their credit card, and you'll still have to provide significant documentation of the need for those expenses and their relation to the cancellation of your flight.
- Most credit card companies have a maximum amount of expenses they will reimburse, and not every expense will qualify even if your total is below that threshold.
- For example, your credit card company may be willing to reimburse food expenses for meals you had to eat at the airport as a result of a flight cancellation or delay, but it may balk at covering a dinner you ate at a five-star restaurant downtown after learning your flight was canceled.

Method 3

Buying Travel Insurance

1. Compare policies in advance. Look at the prices and coverage levels of several different travel insurance policies before you commit to one.

- If you plan to buy travel insurance, you should purchase it either on the same day you book your trip or as soon afterward as possible.
- If you travel frequently, you may want to consider a multi-trip or annual policy, which can save you both time and money compared to purchasing travel insurance for each trip separately.
- Different policies cover travel for different lengths of time, and cover different types of risks. Typically the more risks are covered, the more expensive the policy will be.
- You may want to check with a third-party such as a travel agent or a travel website if you're unsure about different types of policies.
- You also should consider talking to friends, particularly if you know someone who is a frequent traveler or who just returned from a trip similar to the one you want to take. In addition to their recommendations, their stories can help you assess the risks you might encounter on your trip.

2. Choose the policy that best meets your needs. Which policy is the best fit for you will depend on where you're going, how long you'll be gone, and the reasons for your trip.

- The policy that will work best for you also depends on how much risk you are willing to take. That may fluctuate depending on where you plan to travel. For example, you may want more comprehensive coverage if you're planning a safari in Africa than you would want if you were visiting Toronto for a week to stay with friends.
- Travel insurance may go beyond compensation for canceled flights to include medical or legal expenses as well as coverage for personal liability while you're on your trip.

3. Keep in touch with your carrier. Once you've purchased your travel insurance policy, make sure you update your carrier if any plans or details change that might affect your coverage.

- You typically must notify your carrier if you change travel plans, particularly the date of your departure or locations you plan to visit.
- You also should notify your carrier if you expand your trip, causing your travel expenses to increase significantly, as the cost of your trip typically affects the maximum amount your policy covers.
- Additionally, your policy is designed to cover your trip based on the costs you provide. Any difference between the actual cost and the figures you gave your insurance company can result in a claim being denied.

4. Preserve receipts and documentation. Review the claim forms and information before your trip begins so you have a sense of the types of information your carrier requires to process a claim.

- You typically will need information about your trip including your dates of travel, as well as copies of receipts for any expenses you incurred as result of the cancellation.
- If your flight is delayed or canceled, contact the airline and ask for a verification letter. The insurance company may require it to process your claim.

5. File your claim as soon as possible. Your claim is less likely to be denied if you file it soon after your flight is canceled, rather than racking up additional expenses.

- Travel insurance companies typically only cover a certain amount of related expenses per day, so it's in your best interest to mitigate your damages to the extent possible.

- When you file your claim, make sure you've included all requested information and documentation.

How to Transfer Travel Reward Points to Another Program

Many credit card companies and airline loyalty programs offer travelers the chance to earn reward points and transfer them into discounted airline tickets, rental cars, and hotel stays. Some programs will allow you to send your points to another travel program. If you are frequently on the go, participating in these programs may be a great way to save money. Before you redeem your travel points, review the details of your program contract. Each program has different terms and conditions for accruing, using, and transferring points. Understanding your redemption choices and knowing how to transfer your travel points can help you select the best option for you.

Part 1

Transferring Travel Reward or Loyalty Points

1. Phone your program's customer service department. Credit cards, airline credit cards, and loyalty programs will provide a customer service department phone number, which is typically listed on the back of the credit or membership card or on your monthly statement. A customer service representative can help transfer your reward points to another travel program that they are partnered with. They can also share your available point balance and help you initiate the transfer.

   - Be sure to have your account number available. You can typically find this on your membership card or on listed on your monthly statements.

- You must be the primary account holder or an authorized member that is linked to the account to transfer points to another program.

2. Transfer your rewards online. Most credit card companies and loyalty programs will provide you with access to your statements, transfer options, and redemption choices on an online portal or app. Once you have signed into your account, look for a section that references your credit card or membership points, such as "Redeem My Rewards," or "Use or Transfer My Points." Click through to this section to review begin your transfer.

- Travel programs that have partnered with your loyalty program can change without notification. Be sure to review what programs are currently available to you. The online portal will have the most up-to-date information regarding partnership programs.

3. Pay attention to transfer fees. A point transfer fee may be applied when you transfer your points to another program. These fees vary from program to program, and some do not charge a fee at all. For example, you can be charged up to $30 dollars to transfer points from an American Express card to their partnered airline. Before the transaction is completed, you will have a chance to review and agree to a transfer fee.

- Review your contract or talk to a representative online or over the phone to see if you will be required to pay a transfer fee.

Part 2

Considering your Transfer Options

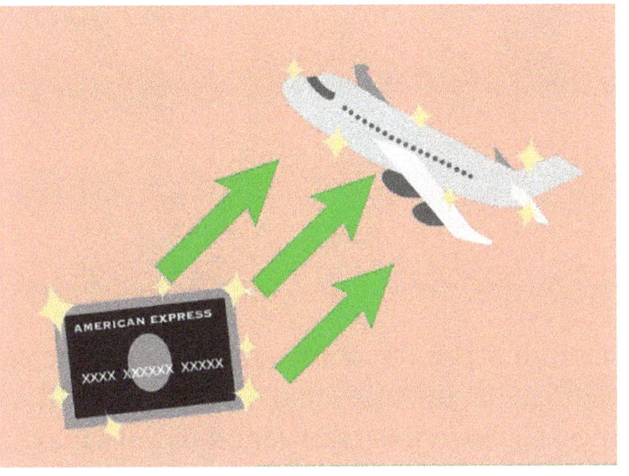

1. Send your credit card points to an airline program. Some credit card programs will allow you to transfer your earned, but not redeemed, credit card points to an airline loyalty program. For many credit cards, you can earn 1 mile for 1 credit card point. Some cards, like American Express Membership Rewards and Chase Ultimate Rewards, offer same-day or 24-hour transfers. Other programs may take up to a week.

- To increase your chances of earning a free airline ticket, save your credit card points and send them to the airline program of your choice.

2. Book tickets and accommodations with your travel points. Consider using your travel reward points to book future tickets and hotels. You can earn points and receive discounts if you use your points to pay for plane tickets, hotel bookings, a rental car, or travel excursions. In some cases, you and your spouse or domestic partner can combine your points if you both have the same credit card. Review your contract or chat with a representative to see if this is an option for you.

- Chase Sapphire Preferred or Ink Plus cardholders can receive a discount up to 20% when they use points to book accommodations or airline tickets by using their accrued points.

3. Gift your travel miles to another person. Some airline loyalty programs allow you to transfer your accrued miles to another person, provided that that person holds a membership account with that airline. Delta, for instance, allows you to send your miles to a maximum of 4 individuals. If you would like to send your miles to someone else, you must provide that person's name and account number to complete the transaction.

- You must have a certain number of miles before you can gift them to another loyalty program member. Most airlines require a minimum of 1,000 miles before a transfer can take place.
- Gifting your miles to another member typically cannot be canceled once the transaction is completed.

Part 3

Collecting Transferable Travel Loyalty Points

1. Join a frequent-flier program. Airline rewards programs can be beneficial to a frequent traveler. These programs ensure customer loyalty by providing incentives to individuals to fly exclusively with that airline or a group of airlines. When choosing a program, consider the airline's flight options, your particular travel needs, the program's benefits, and how easy it is to earn a free or discounted flight.

- If you travel to a particular area for work or to visit family, find out if an airline's headquarters are located in a nearby airport. There will be more flight options in and out of an airline's home base. For example, British Airways is based in London, while Delta airlines is based out of Atlanta.

- There are currently three major airline loyalty programs to choose from, which include One World, Sky Team, and Star Alliance. American Airlines, for instance, is a member of One World, as are Qatar Airways, Etihad Airlines, and other United Arab Emirates airlines. If you travel to the Middle East frequently, it may be best to join this frequent-flier program.

2. Sign up for a hotel-loyalty program. If you travel frequently, consider signing up for a hotel-loyalty program. These programs allow you to accrue points for staying at particular hotels within their network. You can transfer your collected program points to a variety of other programs, including airline programs or car rental agencies.

- Priority Club Rewards, an international hotel loyalty program, allow you to exchange your points for airline miles with most major American airlines at the rate of 4 points for 1 mile. Starwood Preferred Guest allows you to exchange 1 point for 1 mile for most airlines.
- RewardsPlus is a partnership between Marriott hotels and United Airlines. This program allows you to collect points when you stay at a Marriott hotel or fly with United, and it allows you to easily transfer and redeem your loyalty points for travel or accommodations. Occasionally, this program offers bonus points when you convert points between programs.

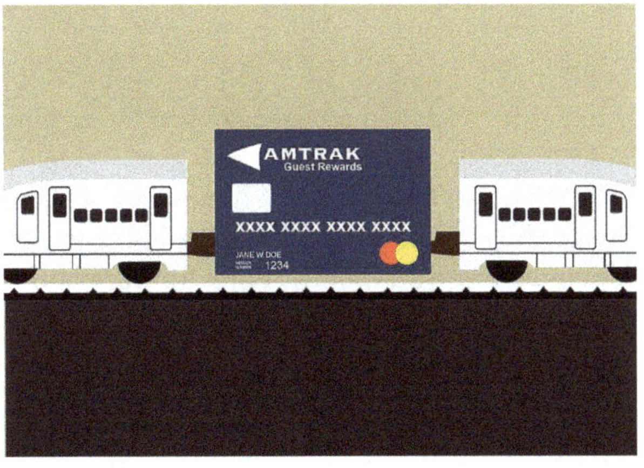

3. Enroll in a rider-rewards program. Rider programs offer perks and discounts to reward frequent travelers and to draw in new customers. If you frequently take a train or a bus line, check to see if that company or organization has a loyalty program.

- The Amtrak Guest Rewards program allows you to transfer your points collected by using Amtrak train services. You can transfer these points to rewards programs with their hotel partners, Hilton, La Quinta, and Wyndham, or exchange them for United Airlines miles.

How to Choose Cheap Train Travel

Choosing cheap train travel is easy if you know how. Before buying tickets, you should know where you want to go. Look for routes that take a longer, more circuitous route to your destination – they're often cheaper than the direct trains. Book as far in advance as possible – unless you want to try to snatch a super-cheap ticket at the last minute. Take advantage of any discounts for veterans, children, and students that the rail lines offer. Shop around and look at several different rail companies and routes before deciding which tickets you want to buy.

Method 1

Mapping your Trip

1. Buy the individual legs of your ticket separately. When people order train tickets, they tend to purchase a ticket on a straight shot to wherever they're going. But strangely, buying tickets for every step along the journey could save you money. Look for opportunities to engage in so-called "ticket-splitting" where possible.

- For instance, suppose you're taking a train from Washington, D.C. to New York City. The train will also pass through Baltimore and Philadelphia. If you buy three tickets – one from D.C. to Baltimore, another from Baltimore to Philadelphia, and a third from Philly to New York – you could save money when comparing the cost to buying a single ticket for a trip from D.C. to New York.
- Check the prices on the split tickets to ensure that they total less than what you'd pay for the single ticket.

2. Take the scenic route. Popular routes are direct and travel quickly to their destination. But they are also the most expensive tickets. Look for less popular routes which are less direct. It might take you longer to arrive at your destination, but you might save on ticket fare.

3. Sign up for alerts. Some railway ticket retailers offer customers the opportunity to get alerts sent to their phone or email. Trainline, for instance, will ping your email when tickets go on sale to a location you've confirmed an interest in. Other train ticket retailers offer similar alert systems. Contact the rail line of your choice to find out how you can get alerted when tickets for destinations you're interested in are on discount.

Method 2

Saving Money

1. Inquire about discounts. Some rail companies offer travel discounts for certain passengers. Children under the age of seven or eight, for instance, often ride free. Students, military personnel, and seniors might qualify for discounts of varying percentages. Ask the rail company you're booking with if any such discounts exist, and claim discounts that apply to you.

2. Check for cheap first-class tickets. Strangely, first-class tickets are often cheaper than economy

or standard fare tickets. This tends to be the case on trains where all the standard class fares have been sold. And if you get a first-class ticket on the cheap, you're in double luck – you've saved money and you get all the amenities of first-class fare.

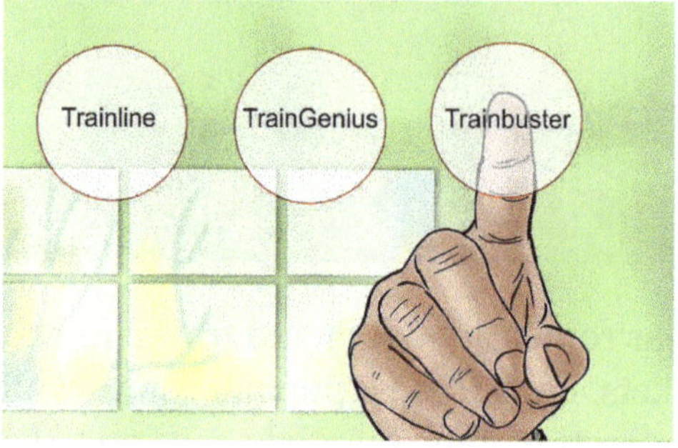

3. Shop around. There are lots of routes with more than one rail company operating on them. Look at all the companies operating in your area and choose the one that best matches your budget and schedule.

- Use a metasearch engine like Trainline, TrainGenius, or Trainbuster to find all the possible routes and lines heading to your destination.

4. Compare prices for single tickets against the price of a round-trip ticket. If you're traveling to a destination and back again, and if you know exactly when you want to return, you might be tempted to book a round-trip fare. However, round-trip tickets can be more expensive than two one-way tickets bought at different times.

- Waiting to buy your return trip ticked is a gamble. You might end up paying more for the second ticket than for the first. You might also not be able to get a return fare if you wait too long to obtain it.

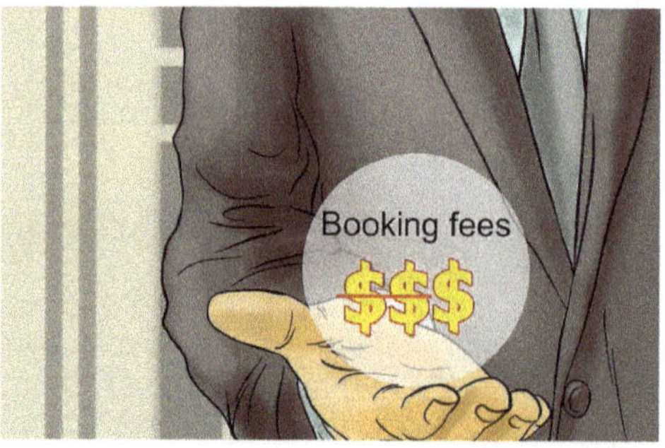

5. Look for low booking fees. When booking online or over the phone, you'll have to pay an addi-

tional fee – the booking fee – to reserve your ticket. These fees range from modest to exorbitant, depending on which rail company you're dealing with. If you don't see the booking fees automatically represented when you're going to check out, contact the rail line directly to find out what the full cost of the tickets you want will be.

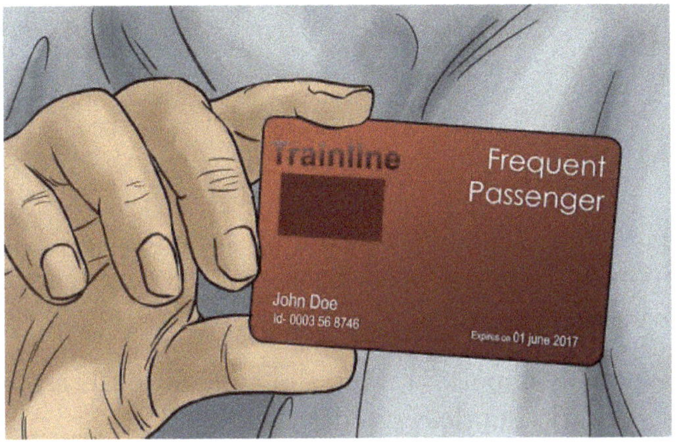

6. Get a frequent passenger card. If you travel often by rail, you might qualify for the train equivalent of the "frequent flyer" card. Many rail companies offer discounted fare for repeat customers who have a frequent passenger card. Contact your rail company of choice to see if any such offer is available.

Method 3

Choosing When to Travel

1. Avoid peak travel times. Tickets are often priced according to the time of day when the train runs. Most people want to travel by train between 4:00 and 7:00 in the evening, or any time in the morning prior to 10:00. Therefore, tickets for trips that operate during those times are often priced more expensively than off-peak times. If you're in no particular rush to arrive at your destination, look for tickets at different times of day to locate off-peak tickets that can save you money.

- Sundays and Fridays are also peak travel times, since the rail lines tend to attract people traveling somewhere or other for the weekend on Friday, then returning Sunday from wherever they went.

2. Buy your tickets early. Railway companies tend to jack their prices up as the date of departure draws closer. In order to avoid getting gouged, book your tickets as soon as you know when you want to leave and where you want to go.

- Buying early is especially important when shopping for deals around holidays. When lots of people are traveling, ticket prices rise dramatically.

3. Buy your tickets at the last minute. While it is good practice to buy your tickets early, you might, paradoxically, be able to get your tickets cheap if you buy them at the last possible moment. This is because when the train departs the station with empty seats, the rail company has no way to recoup the costs of the unsold tickets. Therefore, they attract late-coming customers by steeply discounting unsold tickets.

- However, if you choose to buy your tickets at the last minute, there's a good chance that the tickets will all be sold out. Therefore, it is best to plan ahead and buy your train tickets well in advance of your planned date of departure.

4. Be flexible in your travel arrangements. Rail companies often price their tickets in seemingly

inexplicable ways. For instance, tickets to Detroit might cost $50 for a Wednesday trip, but $30 for a Thursday trip. If you do not urgently need to get to Detroit on Wednesday, check for tickets on adjacent days. If you have the good luck to find cheaper tickets on a different day, think about pushing your schedule back to take advantage of the lower rates.

How to Save Money when Booking a Cruise

Saving money on a cruise can be done by using some well known tricks of the trade. As long as you're prepared to plan ahead and make some small sacrifices to your cabin arrangements, you should find you can make considerable savings and still have an amazing cruise experience.

Steps

1. Book in advance. The longer you can book your cruise trip in advance, the better. You will save considerable amounts by doing so, up to 30 to 40 percent. If possible, try to book a year ahead for the best savings.

2. Book as a group. You are more likely to make savings as a group booking or a large family booking than as an individual, pair or small family. Consider linking up with friends or neighbors, or go for an event such as a wedding, anniversary or graduation.

- Events such as weddings, etc., tend to have good promotional prices for the package deal.

3. Book in low season. This will provide a good discount, as less people will be traveling. However, be well aware of the climatic conditions at the destination ports and be properly dressed before disembarking.

4. Take a lower deck cabin. Higher deck cabins are usually the most expensive ones. Moreover, sea views are usually obtained at a surcharge, along with balconies and access to outside decks from the cabin. You'll save a lot more by remaining on the medium to low areas of the ship decks and by not getting a sea view. You can go up and see the sea any time you like.

5. Book directly on the site of the cruise ship company, or at least check it against other sites. You may find it cheaper than using search engines or other travel sites.

CHAPTER

4

Managing Hotel Reservations

The travel agent must keep in mind the choices and tastes of the customer along with the ambience and services provided by the hotel while making reservations. The customer's budget is an important factor while booking hotels. Hotel reservation management is best understood in confluence with the major topics listed in the following chapter.

How to Get the Best deal Booking a Hotel

Do you want to get the best rate possible on hotel rooms? Different guests staying in the same hotel in identical rooms are likely paying very different prices. Make sure you are paying the best price.

Part 1

Using Traveling Sites

1. Use an opaque travel site. These offer the best price. Many modern opaque sites will allow you too choose everything you want by showing you the best deals.

2. Search for hotel deals on major travel sites. Enter the location and arrival and departure dates,

and then browse the results. You can often narrow the results by free accommodations, cost, and rating. Motels and inns are often cheaper than hotels, and free breakfasts are usually cost- and time-efficient.

- Major travel sites. You can also compare all the major travel sites at once with hotel comparison sites. You can even compare hotels within each site by checking the box next to hotels you like and then clicking on the 'Compare' button. This way, you will have page view of three hotels side-by-side that you can also print for later review. Some hotels do not include free internet, breakfast etc. That can be seen using this 'Compare' feature.

3. Check one of the "Hotel Search Engines". These sites are very popular today. They allow you to instantly search hundreds of different travel websites and then post the lowest rates. Using these search engines to find and sort hotel rates can save time and money. Don't forget to check DealAngel to make sure the rate you book is actually a bargain.

4. Join a members-only club for special deals. These sites can offer lower prices because the rates aren't available to the general public. Vacationist is a members-only site that holds special sales on luxury hotels around the world. Hotel Engine is a members-only site that offers discounted rates on a ton of hotels and claims to beat the prices found on other sites most of the time. Membership in both clubs is free.

5. Use any flexibility you might have. If you are flexible about the date of your stay, investigate different days of the week or an alternative week.

Part 2

Choosing the Right Hotel

1. Consider price and fanciness. If the hotel is merely a place to stay, consider a motel or inn instead, with a free continental breakfast so you can continue with your trip quickly. If you'll be staying at the hotel with loved ones for two or more days, consider spending more for nicer stays.

2. Consider location. Sometimes it will pay off to pay more for a hotel nearer your destination.

3. Consider accommodations. These include free breakfasts, Wi-Fi, elevators, and swimming pools. Most places offer a free breakfast and Wi-Fi, both make your stay more convenient and efficient.

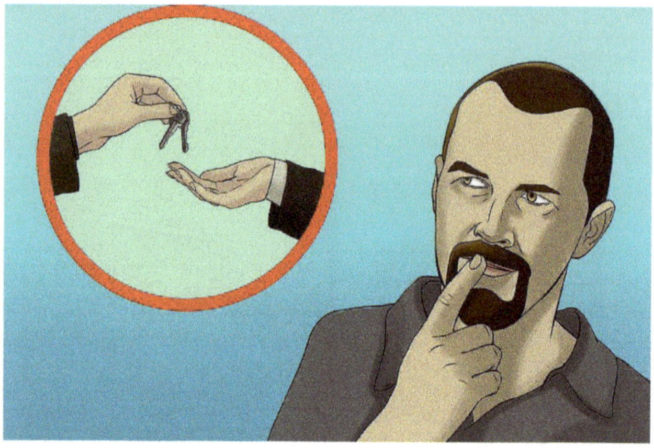

4. Keep the hotel's cancellation policy in mind.

Part 3

Getting the Best Deal on the Hotel

1. Go directly to the hotel's website. Investigate the prices on the site. Do they have any specials? Sign up to be notified of any specials by email. Note the prices for the date you'll be traveling.

2. Call the hotel directly, and negotiate with them for the best deal.

- Tell them you are interested in getting a good deal. When they say the price, make a counter offer and take a hard line when negotiating. Most hotels will offer very good deals for the night after 6:00 P.M. if they have a lot of unsold inventory (otherwise the revenue will be lost on those rooms). After 8:00 P.M., you may be able to negotiate to a 75% discount, especially with smaller, owner-managed, hotels.
- Ask for any discounts. Most places don't advertise the discounts, but will offer them upon being asked. There are multiple types of discounts, so see if you'll qualify for one or two of them:
  - Automobile association cards
  - Senior rates
  - Entertainment cards
  - Business traveler rates
  - Government/veteran rates
  - Discounts for booking more than one room, or staying more than one night.
- Ask if the hotel will match its price with a cheaper hotel of similar quality.

3. Book your room. After you've gathered the details, you can book your room and be confident that you are getting the best rate possible.

4. Negotiate your rate at the hotel. If you are a walk-in guest (meaning you don't have reservations at the hotel) take advantage of the front desk staff. Tell them you're only looking for a place to sleep, and ask them for the best deal they can give you. Chances are, they'll lower their advertised price in order to keep you from walking out the door. Most hotels are willing to negotiate their rates down by about $20. In the eyes of the business, selling a room for $20 less than planned is better than not selling the room at all.

5. Ask for an upgrade. If a hotel isn't full, you can often get an upgraded room, like a king bed or corner room, just by asking. This may not save money, but it will get you more for the money you are spending.

How to Find a Cheap Motel or Hostel

Finding inexpensive accommodations may take a bit of work, but it is possible.

Steps

1. Get a travel guide for your destination. Publishers like Rough Guide, Let's Go and Lonely Planet usually write travel books targeted to younger travelers and include lists of cheap places to stay.

2. Check out Hostelling International online. They run affordable, comfortable hostels worldwide.

3. See if there is a YWCA or YMCA at your destination that provides beds for travelers.

4. Some schools offer accommodations to their alumni, such as the Harvard Club, the worldwide network of Sacred Heart schools etc. Check to see if your college does the same.

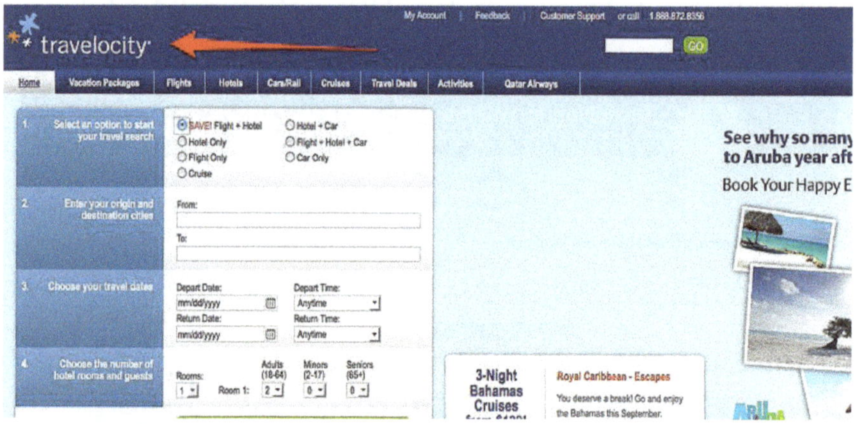

5. Try discount travel sites like Orbitz, Travelocity etc.

6. Subscribe to weekly travel discount online mailing lists such as Sherman's or Travelzoo.

7. Read Arthur Frommer's Budget Travel.

8. Google "cheap hotels [name of destination]".

9. Look at travel blogs and travel website.

How to Book a Travel Homestay

A travel homestay is a great way to save money and immerse yourself in local culture. Choosing a homestay instead of a hotel means you will have expanded opportunities to experience your travel destination from a local perspective. Before booking a travel homestay, make sure you are utilizing a reputable agency, have contacted the host's references, and have asked the host important questions about the homestay.

Method 1

Choosing the Right Travel Homestay

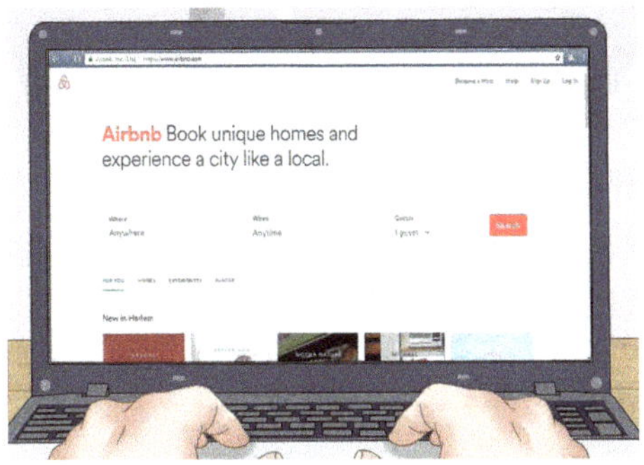

1. Utilize a reputable agency. Your best bet for a safe and successful travel homestay is to book it through a reputable agency, company, or website. You should choose an agency that has been booking homestays in your destination for a considerable period of time and has high ratings from customers. Reputable resources for booking travel homestays include:

- Airbnb
- CouchSurfing
- Homestay
- Servas

2. Try the local tourism board. If you can't find information on a homestay in your travel destination from a reputable homestay resource, you can try contacting the local tourism board or chamber of commerce. These entities will often have lists of homestays in the region, or may be able to connect you to families and individuals offering homestays in your destination.

3. Read online reviews. If you are booking your travel homestay through a reputable online agency

or company, read online reviews of your host. Many sites, like airbnb.com, have built-in review systems that allow you to read reviews of your potential hosts. Pay attention to bad reviews, even if there is only one of them.

4. Ask for references before booking. You should always ask for references from other travelers before booking a homestay. If the booking agency does not have a built-in review system, ask for contact information of former guests and contact them yourself. Do not rely on the agency to send you written reviews from former guests. Make sure you contact former guests yourself.

5. Talk to friends and family. If you have friends, family, or acquaintances who have previously traveled to your destination, reach out to them. Ask them where they stayed, and if they have suggestions for you. Sometimes the best travel homestays are found by talking to those already within your networks.

6. Meet with your school's study abroad department. If you are a student seeking a travel homestay, you should take advantage of resources at your school. Chances are your school has existing homestay networks in your destination of choice. They can also connect you to other students that have had successful travel homestay experiences in the region to which you will be traveling.

Method 2

Arranging the Details

1. Ask questions about your host family. Before booking your travel homestay, you will want to have a good idea of who your hosts are and precisely who will be living in the house or on the property with you. Email your hosts or message them through your booking agent and ask:

- Who are the people who live in the house?
- How old are they?
- What languages do they speak?
- Will there be other boarders in the house or on the property?
- Who, exactly, will be there during my stay?

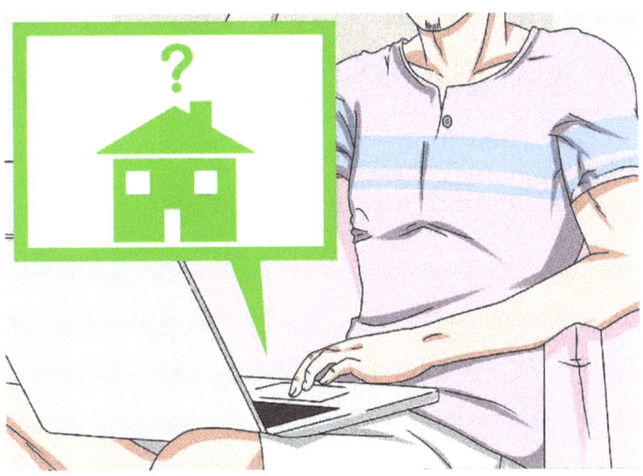

2. Ask your hosts questions about the home. The last thing you want to encounter on your excursion are accommodations that are not what you expected. Before you book your travel homestay, email your host or send them a secure message through your booking agency or site. Questions you should ask include:

- What type of shower is in the home?
- Does the shower have hot water?

- Where is the toilet located?
- What type of heat does the home have?
- Does the home have air conditioning?
- Does the home have fans?
- Are there animals on the property?

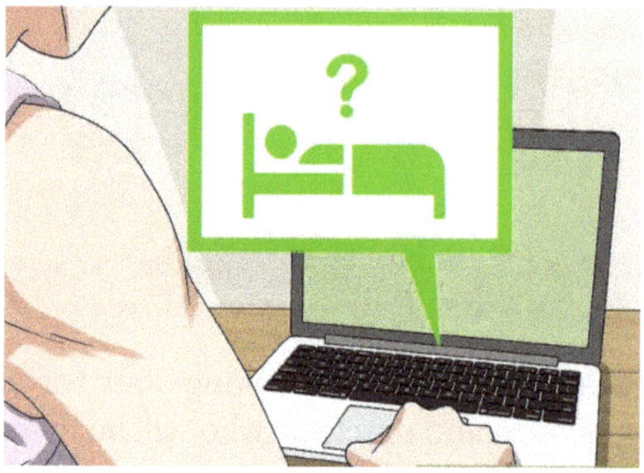

3. Ask about your sleeping arrangements. Before you solidify your travel plans, you will want to ask important questions about where you will be sleeping. Getting a better picture of sleeping arrangements can help you decide if a particular homestay is a good fit for you. If possible, request your hosts send you photographs. Email your hosts and ask:

- What type of room will I be sleeping in?
- Will I be sharing the room or will it be private?
- Whom will I be sharing a room with?
- What type of bed will I be sleeping on?
- Do I need to bring my own bedding?
- Is there a secure place in the room for my belongings?

4. Make sure your dietary needs will be met. Before you decide on a travel homestay, take the time to ask your hosts important questions about the meals you will be eating while staying with them.

This is especially important if you have special needs, such as food allergies or dietary restrictions. Email your host family and ask:

- Are meals included in the homestay?
- Can specific dietary needs be accommodated?

5. Identify your access to phone and Internet. While you are residing at your travel homestay, it is important to identify ahead of time what your access to communication via phone and/or the Internet will be. Do not assume that there will be Wi-Fi on site simply because your host is using the Internet to book your homestay. Contact your host and ask:

- Is there Internet access in the home?
- Will I have access to a phone in the home?
- If I won't have access to phone or Internet in the home, where is the nearest place I can access each and how would I get there from the home?

6. Ask your host about transportation. It's important to know how close your potential travel homestay is to transportation. Contact your host and ask specific questions about where the homestay is located in relation to bus, train, and air transport. Questions to ask include:

- How close in the nearest bus stop?
- How far away from the home is the airport?
- Do taxis come near the residence?
- How long does it take to walk to the train or bus station?

7. Stay in communication with your host. After you book your travel homestay, make sure you stay in communication with your host. This is especially important in the weeks and days leading up to your arrival. You will want to make sure you have a way on contacting your host once you arrive at your travel destination in case any issues arise.

Method 3

Avoiding Common Mistakes

1. Understand you will be a guest in someone's home. Booking a travel homestay means you will be sleeping in the home or on the property of someone who lives in your travel destination. You might have little personal space, and will be asked to abide by the rules of the household. You might even be expected to help with cooking and cleaning tasks, depending on your arrangement.

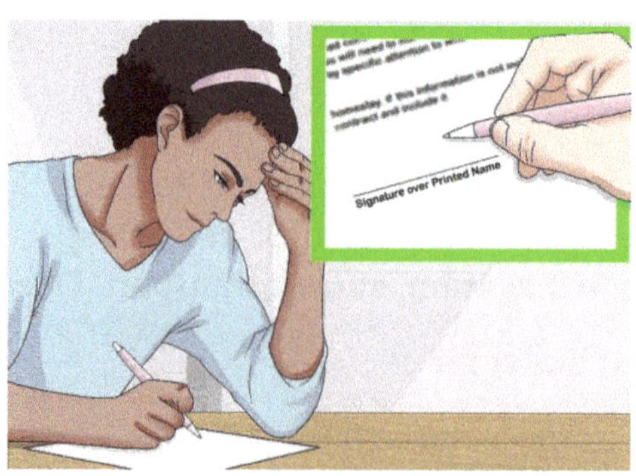

2. Read contracts carefully before signing. Before you book your travel homestay, you will need to make sure you read the fine print. Read every word of all contracts. Pay specific attention to what

your recourse is should you become unhappy with your homestay. If this information is not included, ask your host or agency to amend the contract and include it.

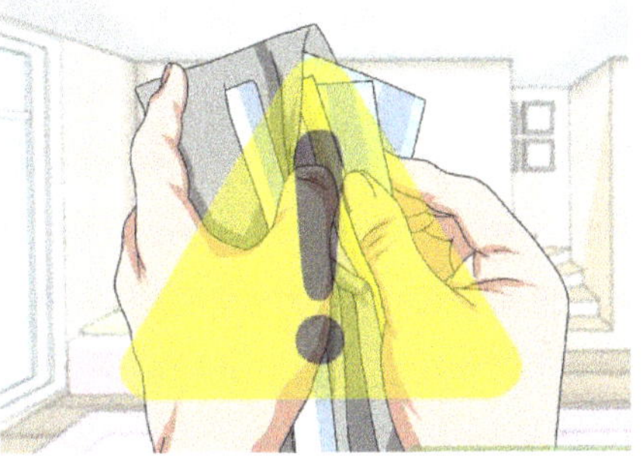

3. Beware of paying in advance. If possible, you should not pay the full balance of your travel homestay before arriving at your destination. This is especially important if you have not seen current photos of the dwelling or read recent reviews. Ask your host for an arrangement that allows you to pay a deposit ahead of time, and then pay the balance upon your arrival.

4. Make safety a priority. When you book a travel homestay, you should make sure that safety is a priority. For example, if you are a single woman, you should avoid homestays where you will be staying alone with a male host. You should also take the location and its safety into consideration. For example, you should not book a travel homestay that is too far away from public transportation or forms of communication such as telephone or Internet service.

5. Trust your instincts. Whether you are in the booking process, or have already arrived at your travel homestay, you must always follow your instincts. If your gut is telling you a situation is unsafe, or a homestay seems too good to be true, it probably is. Remove yourself from the situation immediately if your instincts tell you that you should.

Method 4

Considering the Benefits of a Travel Homestay

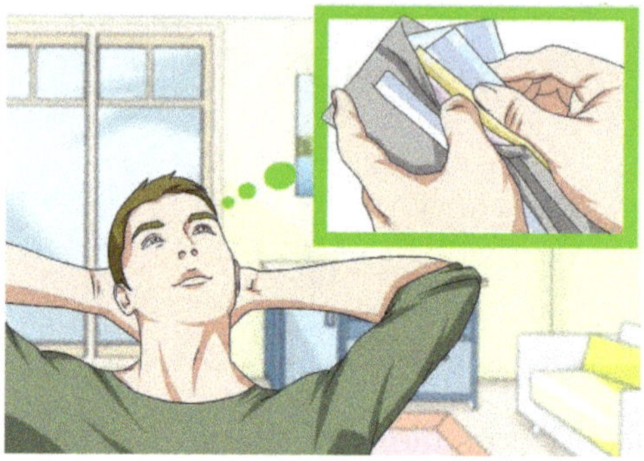

1. Think about the financial incentive. One of the benefits of booking a travel homestay for your next trip is economic. In general, a travel homestay will be cheaper than a modern hotel room in your travel destination. The economic benefits of a travel homestay increase if you are planning a more extended stay on your next trip.

2. Consider cultural immersion. When you book a travel homestay, you will likely be interacting with your hosts on a regular basis. This means you will be communicating and eating with locals. This can provide opportunities to become more immersed in the local culture than is afforded by more traditional hotel lodging.

3. Think about language opportunities. One of the possible benefits of a travel homestay comes in the form of language. When you are living with or near local people, you will have more opportu-

nities to learn and practice the local language. This can be especially beneficial if you plan on being in a region or a country for an extended period of time.

4. Don't forget about the food! When you arrange for a travel homestay, there is a good chance you will have an opportunity to eat with your hosts. This means you will get to enjoy local food as prepared by local people, rather than food you might find in restaurants near hotels that are geared toward tourists. Some travel homestay hosts might even provide you with an opportunity to learn how to prepare local food!

5. Decide if a travel homestay is right for you. Travel homestays are not for every traveler. If you value privacy, anonymity, and personal space, a travel homestay might not be the best accommodation choice for you. Home stays are also not usually the best choice for those with limited travel time, as many homestays have a minimum length of stay that can range from 3 days to several weeks.

How to Find Cheap Hotels

Hotels regularly sell their under booked rooms for less than their standard price. The Internet is flush with hotel discount websites, so it can be difficult to know which service is listing the lowest price. Although the Internet is still the best place to look for big deals on hotel rooms, you can use all these tools to get the biggest discount.

Method 1

Knowing your Search Tools

1. Expect that most travel aggregate sites search for hotel deals. That does not mean, however, that all the sites will show the same information. Plan to look at three or more sites before you book.

- The hotels listed depends upon what hotels choose to list their under booked rooms and which sites have already sold out of their vacant rooms.

2. Try Kayak. This site claims to find 25 percent or more off a hotel stay. The advantage of Kayak is that it is well known by hotel chains and it allows you to compare a flights, cars and vacations in addition to hotels.

3. Visit websites if you want to find a risk-free reservation. Unlike most hotel chains that make you reserve with your credit card and pay a fee if you cancel, Booking.com allows you to search for listings and review them based on free cancellation.

- You may want to book a hotel on this site, keep your confirmation nearby and cancel if you find a better deal.

4. Search websites for last minute hotel deals. If you have a vacation coming up soon and you have yet to book your hotel, these sites perform well.

5. Go to Trivago to search for cheap hotels using a search engine that includes hotel discount websites, like Hotels, Expedia, Booking, Priceline and Travelocity. It may not list all the hotels that are available, but it will compare sites to find you the best price for popular hotels.

6. Try Hotwire for even bigger discounts. The disadvantage of Hotwire is that you pick by location and find out where you will stay after you book. Hotwire doesn't offer easy cancellation and you are taking a bigger risk than with other sites.

Method 2

Joining Loyalty Programs

1. Call your favorite hotel chain to see if they have a loyalty program. Fairmont, Hilton, Hyatt, Joie de Vivre, Kimpton, Marriott, Starwood and many more hotel chains give their loyal customers perks. Call and quiz the membership customer service line to see what they offer.

- Ask the hotel loyalty program if they offer free Internet. Fancier hotels have stopped providing free Internet to clients. Starwood gives you free Internet upon enrollment.
- Most loyalty programs work on a points system. Once you earn a certain amount of points, you get a free stay. They are best for frequent travelers.

2. Peruse the list of hotel loyalty programs on TravelZoo.

3. Sign up for your loyalty program e-newsletter. They will email you about room sales and you

can book by clicking on the email and booking online. Make sure to compare these sale emails to Booking.com or another aggregate site to ensure you are being offered the best deal.

4. Sign up for an AARP, AAA, or professional association membership. Many of these associations have partnerships with certain hotels. You can expect a 10 to 25 percent discount on certain hotel chains.

Method 3

Packaging your Accommodation

1. Use your airline to book your hotel. You may get a good deal on hotels, hotel transfers, car rentals and more by booking what airlines call a "vacation."

2. Search Expedia, Kayak, Travelocity and other sites for package deals. Travel agents may be offering special deals on flights and hotels to fill their last few empty spots.

3. Click on the section entitled "last minute deals" on each website. You may be able to score a deal by booking an entire vacation (flight and hotel) just a week or two before you plan to travel. You must be extremely flexible.

Method 4

Asking for Discounts

1. Call a hotel or go into a location and haggle for cheaper accommodation. Tell the hotel what price you are looking for. Suggest that you want to check if they want to offer a deal before you try places down the road.

- Unless there is a strict no-discounts policy, most hotel managers will be flexible and give you the rate available on Hotels.com or another site.
- If they won't offer you a discount, ask if they will give you free services like a breakfast or Internet.

2. Ask for an industry discount. Say that you are a representative of your company looking to book

a group of rooms at a hotel in the area. They may call you out or they may give you an industry rate of 10 to 15 percent off or more.

- You should also ask for an educator discount, military discount or a non-profit discount if you are associated with a school, charity or branch of military service.

3. Search Coupon websites if you want to stay at a certain hotel. Search according to the hotel name at Retail Me Not, Coupons.com or Coupon Heaven. If they don't have a discount code, they may have coupons for free Internet or services.

4. Travel in the off-season to find cheaper rates. Europe in the fall or winter and South America or the Caribbean in the summer will have far lower rates than in the high season.

5. Book after 6 pm on the same day of travel. If you are up for adventure and a little risk, wait for

hotels with unbooked rooms to offer discounts. Remember that you must ask or they will charge you the standard rate.

- Leave your luggage in the car when you ask for discounts or haggle. You send the message that you are going to stay at the hotel if you bring your suitcase with you.

How to Find Hotels for a Long Term Stay

Traveling will sometimes keep you in a location for a week or more. Hotels offer a range of options for the traveler who is staying longer. Sorting through a few of these possibilities will help you find the right room for your stay and control costs. If you're interested in trying something new, there are also lodging options you may not have considered.

Part 1

Researching Choices

1. Search for extended-stay hotels. Extended-stay hotels, such as Candlewood Suites, My Place Hotels, and TownePlace Suites offer affordable suites. Compare several extended-stay hotels with websites such as Extended Stay Network or Extended Stay Hotel Network.

2. Look into a traditional hotel. Although they don't offer many of the same benefits as extended-stay

hotels, some traditional hotels do offer suites, small kitchenettes, or breakfast buffets. Opt for one of these hotels if it is the most conveniently located and offers the amenities that are important to you.

3. Contact independent hotels. Whether you choose an extended-stay or a traditional hotel, independent hotels have the greatest flexibility when working with customers. They may offer incentives, such as gift cards, discounts, or a room upgrade, to compete with larger chain hotels. Ask what they have available.

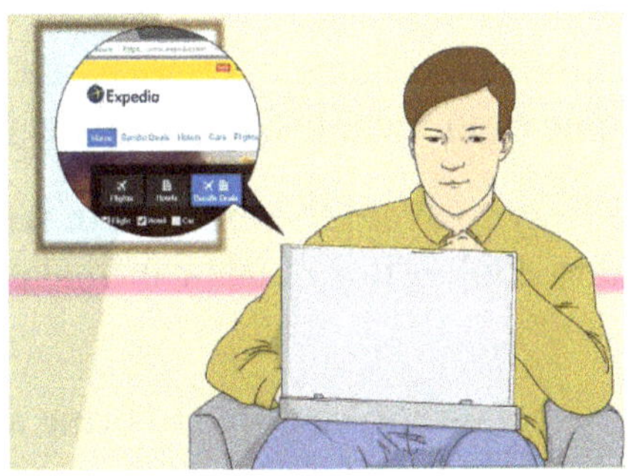

4. Look at third party reservations sites. Check websites such as Expedia, Orbitz, or Hotels.com for lists of nearby hotels and their amenities. These sites offer discounts on reservations, although they are limited in the flexibility they can offer, especially if you need to extend your stay or cut it short. Compare different sites to what the hotel can offer directly to be sure you're getting the best deal.

5. Ask friends and family for recommendations. If you know people who live in the area or have visited there, ask their advice about places to stay. They may have ideas you haven't heard of. People rely on personal recommendations more than any other method of choosing a hotel. Reach out to the people you know.

6. Check out the amenities offered. Extended-stay hotels offer a variety of services that aren't available at traditional hotels. They can be very important when you're away from home. Check if the following amenities are offered:

- Onsite laundry facilities. This is an important convenience, freeing you from finding a laundromat or laundry service.
- Meals that are included in the price. Some hotels include both breakfast and dinner in the cost of their suites, and some even include complimentary cocktails with dinner.
- In-suite kitchens. Another way to avoid the expense of restaurants is to prepare meals for yourself. Also, being able to cook a few meals can make your stay feel a little more like home.
- Pet-friendly facilities. Some hotels allow people to bring along certain animals. Call ahead to make sure your pet is allowed.
- Personal service. Because people stay longer at these hotels, the staff will often get to know them. An extended stay away from home can be lonely, and feeling like a part of a community can help.

Part 2

Getting the Best Deal

1. Make reservations with the hotel. Both extended-stay and traditional hotels can offer the best

deals directly. Call the front desk, rather than making reservations online or through the hotel's 1-800 number. Explain how long your stay will be and see if you can get a percentage off your bill.

2. Inquire about price matching. Hotels will often match a competitor's price. For an extended stay, a price adjustment will add up. If you find a hotel that costs less but have your heart set on a different location, ask if the lower rate can be matched.

3. Use a bidding site. Bid for discounted rooms through sites such as Priceline and Hotwire. You will only know the location of the hotel and its rating when you're picking rooms to bid on. Use this option if you're comfortable with not knowing exactly which hotel you'll be in until after it's booked.

4. Ask your employer about a corporate discount. Your employer may offer discounts at certain hotels as a fringe benefit. Inquire about what is available through work. Compare that discount to other savings opportunities.

Part 3

Finding Alternate Lodging

1. Book a short-term sublet. Check business such as Airbnb or Flipkey, where homeowners offer short-term rentals of their property. Compare prices, space offered, and ratings provided by previous customers. Give yourself time to sort through the choices.

2. Participate in a house exchange. For a membership fee, websites such as Home Exchange and Love Home Swap coordinate opportunities for homeowners to trade houses for vacations. If you're comfortable having others stay in your home, use this to have a full home available for your stay. Research to be sure the options available to you are close enough to your destination.

3. Stay in student housing. For a no-frills but very affordable option during the summer, contact local universities. They will sometimes allow people to rent empty dorm rooms. Try this if you're not looking for lush accommodations.

How to Book a Room at a Historic Hotel

Interested in staying in an antebellum or Victorian hotel? There are minuses, but for the history buff, many pluses.

Steps

1. Check the Internet to see if there are any historic hotels in the city/town you wish to visit.

2. If they have one, visit the website to see pictures of the rooms as well as rates.

3. Before booking a room, check for reviews on travel sites.

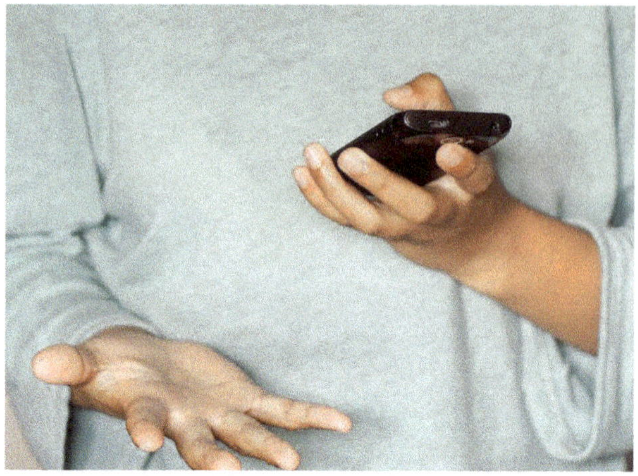

4. Even if they offer online booking, for small, older hotels, calling the front desk to book the reservation is the best bet.

5. Before calling to book the reservation, be sure you know what you want to ask: Is the room I'm requesting on the ground floor or an upper room? Do you have an elevator? Are there coffee makers, blow dryers, irons, etc. in the room?

6. Before booking, ask what the flat total with tax? Ask if there are any other charges that may be accrued.

7. Double check the cancellation policy. Most historic establishments have more stringent cancellation policies than modern establishments do because of fewer rooms. Cancellation policies can range anywhere from seven to thirty days advance notice prior to arrival or else you credit card will be charged.

How to Choose a Luxury Hotel

Booking a luxury hotel is the easy part––it's the finding and choosing prior to the booking that can take hours and even days of investigation. Even when you've found what you think looks like the perfect hotel, how do you know that it's the right one for your needs? Fortunately, it is possible to choose a luxury hotel with the minimum of fuss by knowing what to look out for before proceeding to booking.

Steps

1. Ask the right questions. Find the answers to these questions. If you do not like the answers that you get, try a different hotel.

- Which is the best room in the hotel?
- What is the finest luxury item in the hotel?
- Which dish must you not miss when eating at the hotel? Are there reviews of the dish and/ or the food?

2. Be certain about what you expect from the hotel. Are you wanting to combine business and pleasure? Are you simply after a great vacation? Or are you only staying there during a business trip? Whatever your need, the hotel needs to be able to meet that specific requirement or you will be better off with a different hotel.

- Before you book a hotel, check whether both your "pleasure" and "needs" are met. If you are traveling with your wife and children, or family and friends, reflect upon these two things seriously.
- The things that you must look for include: Indoor pools, children's menu, professional babysitting, in-room refrigerator and other such services.
- There are many people who also look for spa, gym and various laundry services too. Are these important to you?
- On the other hand, if you are traveling alone or for business purposes, then look out for various features such as: Internet access, convenient shuttles, conference rooms or halls for business meetings and e-booking and fax facilities.

3. Choose the hotel according to its location. If you decide to buy a house, then it is important to select and supervise the location. In a similar manner, a hotel's location is crucial. For instance, if you book hotels in a seaside town, then you will definitely look for seaside hotels, not necessarily

one in the center of town. Doing this will let you enjoy a great seaside view, although if you need to get to town, you'll also need to know how to travel there.

4. Be alert to the other things that you must take into consideration. Some of these include:

- How far are the tourist sites from the hotel?
- How far is the airport or the nearest railway station?
- Where the shopping malls are located?

5. Look at the prices with care. Avoid being swayed by the belief that highly priced hotels are the more luxurious ones. This isn't always the case. Moreover, budget prices can sometimes come with nasty additional costs attached that you weren't expecting. To get the price right, consider the following:

- Check at least three hotels located in the same area. Find ones with little price variation. Simply call the hotels and get quotes. You may find many hotels claiming sky-high prices for their services, while there might be few other hotels that are offering standardized services at a reasonable price.
- Take transport into consideration. The hotel might be a bargain but the transport into the city or to the tourist sites might be prohibitive.

6. Look for value for money.

- Does the booking include local taxes, breakfast?
- What is the check out time?
- What are the facilities? If you have children, a pool or garden would be beneficial.
- Are there restaurants or shops such as supermarkets nearby, if you are doing self-catering? Is self-catering supported?
- Look carefully at what is included; sometimes you will save a few dollars, other times you will pay extra for many other services, so check the pros and cons.

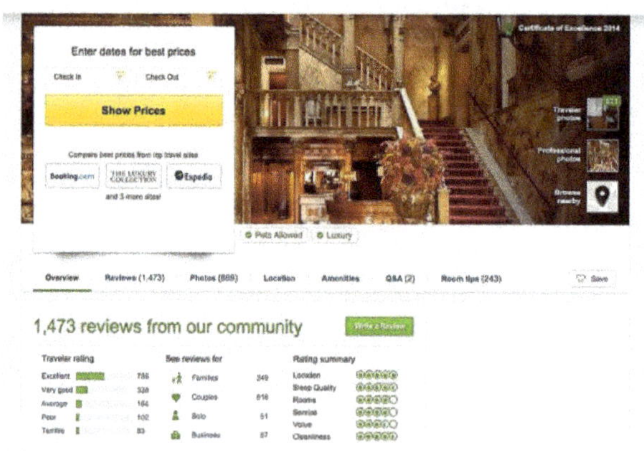

7. Get a sense of the hotel through its website and write-ups. By looking at the feedback, you can get a good idea of what other guests thought about their stay at the place. Are there things that concern you most, such as noise, local nightclub patrons spilling onto the hotel street, cramped rooms, bugs, etc.? Feedback will often bring to light such things and allow you to make an informed decision.

- The best way to find authentic feedback is the reliable travel websites. These websites have records of almost all the hotels in the corner of the world and can bring forth to you valuable opinion from customers who have stayed in a particular hotel.

- Learn to differentiate between the right and the wrong feedback. There are many user reviews which are blatantly positive or overtly negative. For instance, a particular user might have only said positive things about the hotel in question. You might sometimes find it best to disregard really glowing and really negative feedback, in case it was put there by the hotel or its competitors; look for the comments in the middle ground. If you're really unsure, ask the local people or your friends, family and acquaintances about the hotels at the location.

8. Check what events might be occurring in the area at the time of your visit. Perhaps there are discounts, or perhaps the prices skyrocket as a result. If your timing coincides and high prices are unavoidable, it might be worth checking what deals are on offer, to try to save money and enjoy the event as well.

9. Consider whether events held at the hotel itself will disturb your stay. Are there any concerts, karaoke competitions or poolside parties being held during your stay? If large groups of noisy people will be there, it could impact your stay in a negative way. On the other hand, if you're attending too, it might be perfect to stay at the same place.

10. Make your booking. After you have followed the above parts, the next step is to find out more about the best room, the luxury items and the best dish in that particular hotel. If you have completed your research on all this and have taken into account the rates and offerings, you can book with assurance. Then pack your bag and leave on a jet plane for your dream destination. Wishing you a wonderful trip and a luxurious stay in the hotel of your choice.

How to Pay for Online Hotel Bookings

Planning a complete vacation or a business trip can be done efficiently online. Websites such as Expedia, Hotwire, Orbitz, Travoline and Kayak have replaced traditional travel agents in helping people search for and book the least expensive flights, cars and hotel reservations. All major hotel chains provide the opportunity to book a room online, and even international hotels and guest houses are taking reservations through their websites. Pay for online hotel bookings by making a deposit with a credit card, or paying in full for the best rates.

Steps

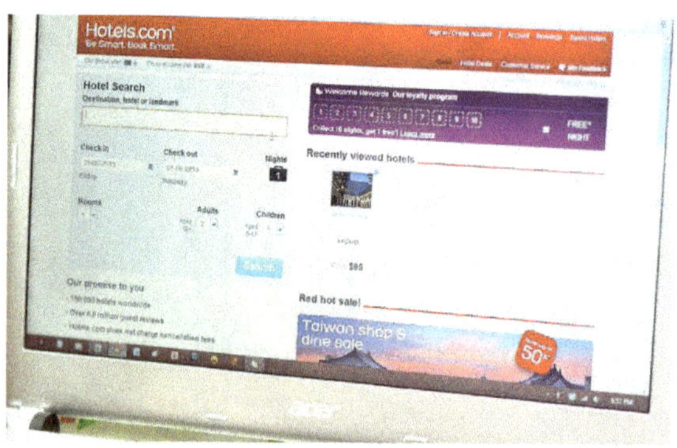

1. Compare prices. Search for the hotel you want by checking specific hotel websites, or using an online travel agent, such as Expedia, Travelocity or Orbitz. Look for hotels that have the dates you need available, and figure out how much you will spend per night.

- Research sites such as Hotels.com or Travelweb, which are specific to hotel bookings only, and do not include additional search options for flights and rental cars.

- Check for additional fees. Some independent online booking agencies charge a fee for using their service. The fee can range from $1 to over $10, and it is never refundable if you cancel or change your reservation.

2. Reserve your hotel. Book the hotel you want by using the hotel's website, or an online travel site. Provide your contact information and the dates you will arrive and check out.

3. Determine when you will have to pay for your booking. As you complete your reservation, you will be given an amount that is due.

- Pay in full for the best rates. Many hotel sites and discount agents will offer you a lower price if you pay for the entire stay at the time of your booking. There are often restrictions on canceling or changing your reservation.

- Provide the required deposit. If your plans may change and you do not want to pay for the full cost of your stay, book a hotel that only requires a deposit. When you pay the deposit required by the hotel, which is often the equivalent of one night's stay, you can usually still change your travel dates without a penalty.

- Pay at the time of your stay. Depending on the hotel, you may be able to guarantee your reservation with a credit card number, but not pay anything until you arrive at the hotel. Most online agents such as Expedia, Orbitz and Hotels.com will not provide this option.

4. Determine how you will pay for your booking.

- Pay by credit or debit card. The easiest way to pay for a hotel booking online is by using a credit card. You will need a credit card number to make a reservation online, and you can use that card to pay for the hotel deposit or the full price of your stay.
- Pay with PayPal, if you want to use BookIt. PayPal is a popular method of online payment, because you do not need to provide your credit card information to yet another website. BookIt is the first online travel agency accepting PayPal as a method of payment. You will need to have a PayPal account already set up.
- Pay with miles or reward points. If you are a frequent traveler, you have probably accumulated enough points at the hotel chain you use to get some nights for free. Book online directly with the hotel, and provide your rewards card number and other information.

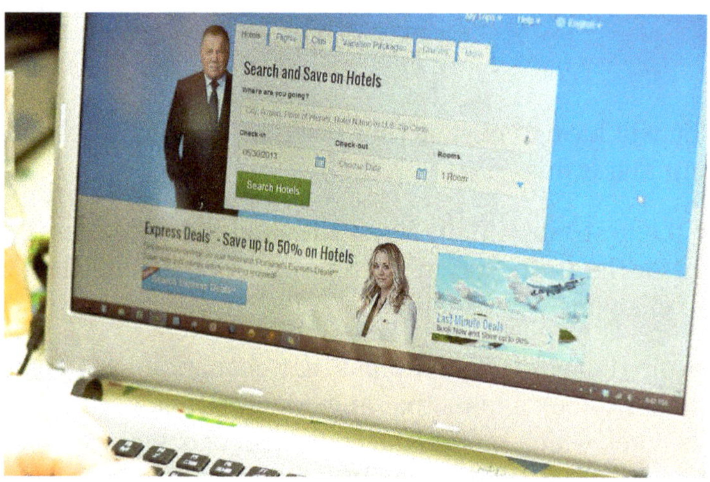

5. Bid on bookings using online auction sites such as Priceline or Hotwire. When you name the price you are willing to pay, you will be given a list of hotel options. Be aware that on sites such as these, you will not always know which hotel you are getting before you book.

- You will need to pay in full with a credit or debit card at the time of booking.

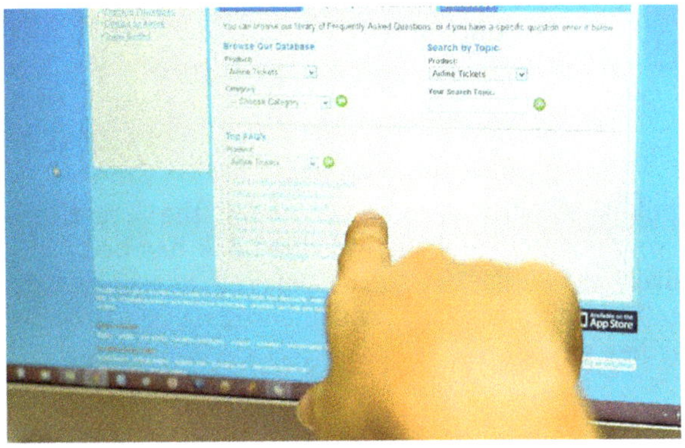

6. Understand the cancellation policy. Some online booking agents such as Priceline and Hotwire do not allow you to change or cancel your reservation at all. Others such as Expedia and Orbitz will charge a fee. If you pay in full, or make a deposit, be sure you read the cancellation policy online. If you are not paying until the time of your stay, find out how far in advance you will need to cancel before your credit card is charged for a night.

Permissions

All chapters in this book are published with permission under the Creative Commons Attribution Share Alike License or equivalent. Every chapter published in this book has been scrutinized by our experts. Their significance has been extensively debated. The topics covered herein carry significant information for a comprehensive understanding. They may even be implemented as practical applications or may be referred to as a beginning point for further studies.

We would like to thank the editorial team for lending their expertise to make the book truly unique. They have played a crucial role in the development of this book. Without their invaluable contributions this book wouldn't have been possible. They have made vital efforts to compile up to date information on the varied aspects of this subject to make this book a valuable addition to the collection of many professionals and students.

This book was conceptualized with the vision of imparting up-to-date and integrated information in this field. To ensure the same, a matchless editorial board was set up. Every individual on the board went through rigorous rounds of assessment to prove their worth. After which they invested a large part of their time researching and compiling the most relevant data for our readers.

The editorial board has been involved in producing this book since its inception. They have spent rigorous hours researching and exploring the diverse topics which have resulted in the successful publishing of this book. They have passed on their knowledge of decades through this book. To expedite this challenging task, the publisher supported the team at every step. A small team of assistant editors was also appointed to further simplify the editing procedure and attain best results for the readers.

Apart from the editorial board, the designing team has also invested a significant amount of their time in understanding the subject and creating the most relevant covers. They scrutinized every image to scout for the most suitable representation of the subject and create an appropriate cover for the book.

The publishing team has been an ardent support to the editorial, designing and production team. Their endless efforts to recruit the best for this project, has resulted in the accomplishment of this book. They are a veteran in the field of academics and their pool of knowledge is as vast as their experience in printing. Their expertise and guidance has proved useful at every step. Their uncompromising quality standards have made this book an exceptional effort. Their encouragement from time to time has been an inspiration for everyone.

The publisher and the editorial board hope that this book will prove to be a valuable piece of knowledge for students, practitioners and scholars across the globe.

Index

CPSIA information can be obtained
at www.ICGtesting.com
Printed in the USA
LVHW060859030122
707669LV00002B/250